FDPE'05

September 25, 2005 • Tallinn, Estonia

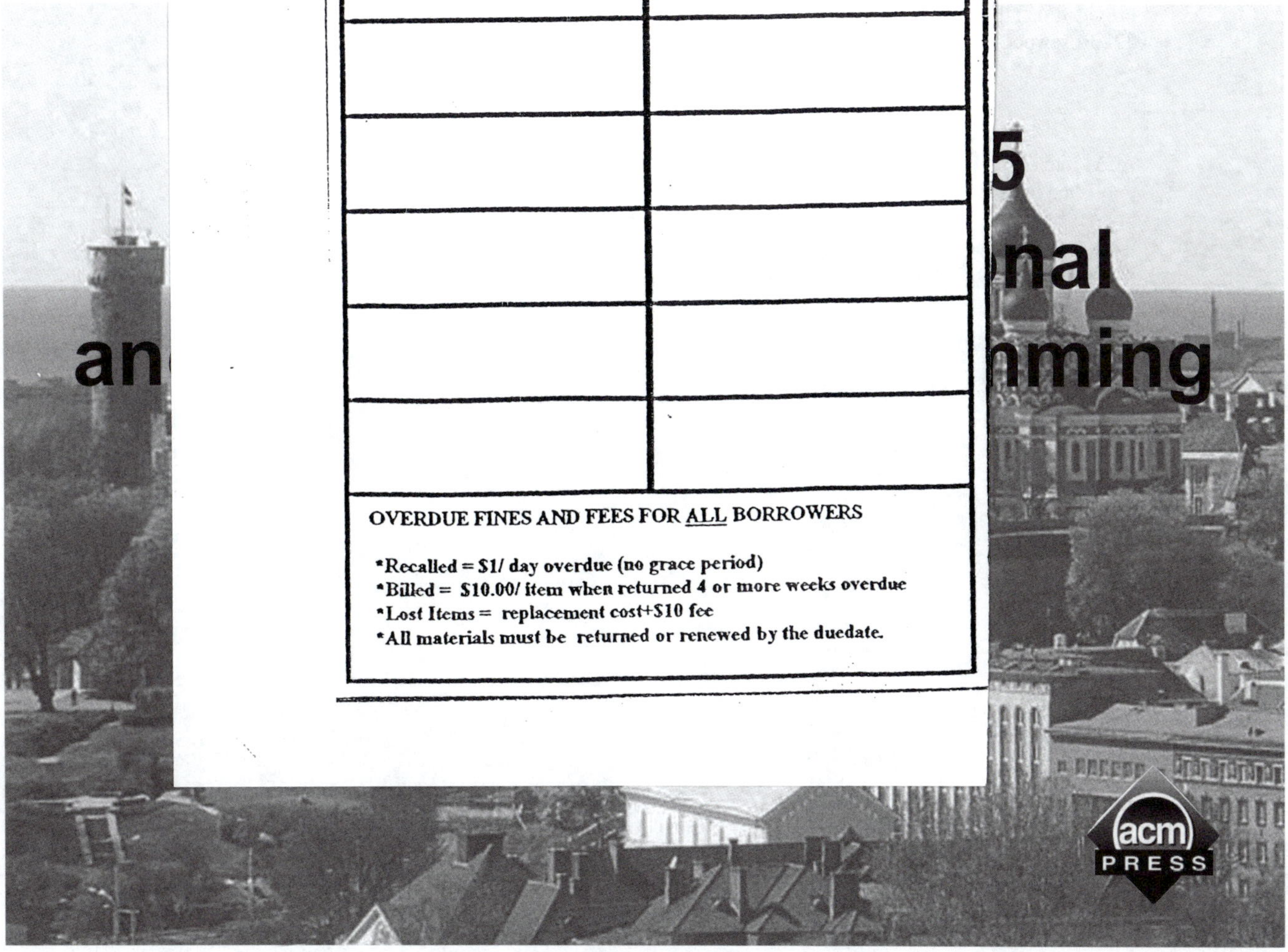

5

nal

an … mming

ACM PRESS

Sponsored by the
Association for Computing Machinery
Special Interest Group on Programming Languages (SIGPLAN)

The Association for Computing Machinery
1515 Broadway
New York, New York 10036

Notice to Past Authors of ACM-Published Articles

ACM intends to create a complete electronic archive of all articles and/or other material previously published by ACM. If you have written a work that has been previously published by ACM in any journal or conference proceedings prior to 1978, or any SIG Newsletter at any time, and you do NOT want this work to appear in the ACM Digital Library, please inform permissions@acm.org, stating the title of the work, the author(s), and where and when published.

ISBN: 1-59593-067-1

Additional copies may be ordered prepaid from:

ACM Order Department
PO Box 11405
New York, NY 10286-1405

Phone: 1-800-342-6626
(US and Canada)
+1-212-626-0500
(all other countries)
Fax: +1-212-944-1318
E-mail: acmhelp@acm.org

ACM Order Number 565056
Printed in the USA

Foreword

The 2005 edition of the *International Workshop on Functional and Declarative Programming in Education (FDPE 2005),* took place in Tallinn (Estonia) on September 25, 2005 as part of International Conference on Functional Programming (ICFP 2005).

Functional and declarative programming plays an increasingly important role in computing education at all levels. This workshop aimed at bringing together educators and others who are interested in exchanging ideas on how to use a functional or declarative programming style in the classroom. Previous workshops have been held in Pittsburgh (2002), Paris (1999), and Southampton (1997). The technical program of the workshop included standard presentations as well as an invited talk on *How to Design Class Hierarchies* by Matthias Felleisen, a *Tips and Tricks* session with contributions from workshop attendees, and a discussion on the links between the FDPE community and that of the Commercial Users of Functional Programming (CUFP).

The organizers reviewed all papers submitted in response to a call for papers. Following the review process and a lively email discussion, the organizers selected the papers contained in these proceedings for presentation at the workshop.

The organizers would like to thank the organization team of ICFP 2005 for hosting the workshop and, in particular, Patricia Johann for her continuous support during the organization.

Robby Findler
The University of Chicago, USA

Michael Hanus
University of Kiel, Germany

Simon Thompson
University of Kent, UK

FDPE 2005 Organizing Committee

Table of Contents

FDPE 2005 Workshop Organization vii

Keynote Address
Session Chair: S. Thompson *(University of Kent)*

- **How to Design Class Hierarchies** 1
  M. Felleisen *(Northeastern University)*

Submitted Papers
Session Chair: R. Page

- **From Functional to Object-Oriented Programming – A Smooth Transition for Beginners** 3
  R. Berghammer, F. Huch *(University of Kiel)*
- **Laziness Without All the Hard Work: Combining Lazy and Strict Languages for Teaching** 9
  E. Barzilay, J. Clements *(Northeastern University)*
- **Word Puzzles in Haskell: Interactive Games for Functional Programming Exercises** 15
  S. A. Curtis *(Oxford Brookes University)*

Submitted Papers
Session Chair: R. Findler *(University of Chicago)*

- **Teaching of Image Synthesis in Functional Style** 19
  J. Karczmarczuk *(Université de Caen)*
- **MinCaml: A Simple and Efficient Compiler for a Minimal Functional Language** 27
  E. Sumii *(Tohoku University)*
- **Engineering Software Correctness** 39
  R. Page *(University of Oklahoma)*

Author Index 47

FDPE 2005 Workshop Organization

Organizing Committee: Robby Findler *(The University of Chicago, USA)*
Michael Hanus *(University of Kiel, Germany)*
Simon Thompson *(University of Kent, UK)*

Sponsor: acm SIGPLAN

Keynote Talk

How to Design Class Hierarchies

Matthias Felleisen
Northeastern University

Abstract

Colleges and universities must expose their students of computer science to object-oriented programming (OOP) even if the majority of the faculty believes that OOP is not the proper programming paradigm for novices. OOP is an important paradigm of thought, and OOP languages are widely used in commercial settings. Ignoring these facts means to ignore the students' needs.

In the past, institutions that introduce functional programming first have explained object-oriented programming via closures and method-oriented dispatch. Put differently, in such courses, students learn to implement objects, message passing, and delegation. They do not learn to design object-oriented programs. Although I firmly believe that our students benefit from such knowledge, I will argue that it is inappropriate as an introduction of object-oriented programming.

My talk will instead present a novel approach to the first-year programming curriculum. Specifically, I will explain how a functional semester ideally prepares students for the true essence of object-oriented programming according to Alan Kay: the systematic construction of small modules of code and the construction of programs without assignment statements. Experience shows that these courses prepare students better for upper-level courses than a year of plain object-oriented programming. Initial reports from our students' co-op employers appear to confirm the experiences of our upper-level instructors.

Biography

Matthias Felleisen is currently a Trustee Professor at Northeastern University. He joined its College of Computer and Information Science in 2001, after a 14-year career at Rice University in Houston with sabbaticals at Carnegie Mellon University in Pittsburgh and École Normale Supérieure in Paris. He received his PhD from Daniel P. Friedman at Indiana University in 1984.

Felleisen's research career consists of two distinct 10-year periods. For the first ten years, he focused on the semantics of programming languages and its applications. His work on operational semantics has become one of the standard working methods in programming languages. For the second ten years, Felleisen and his research group (PLT) developed a novel method for teaching introductory programming, including a new approach to program design and a programming environment for novice programmers (DrScheme). This environment has become a popular alternative to the conventional set of teaching tools and is now used at a couple of hundred colleges and high schools around the world. For Felleisen and his team, the construction of a large, realistic software application has posed many interesting and challenging research problems in programming languages, component programming, software contracts, and software engineering.

Over the past 20 years, Felleisen has published several dozen research papers in scientific journals, conferences, and magazines. In addition, he has co-authored five books, including *How to Design Programs* and *The Little LISPer* (now called *The Little Schemer*), which, at the age of 30, is one of the oldest continuously published books in the field.

FDPE'05, September 25, 2005, Tallinn, Estonia.
ACM 1-59593-067-1/05/0009.

From Functional to Object-Oriented Programming – A Smooth Transition for Beginners

Rudolf Berghammer and Frank Huch

Institute of Computer Science
University of Kiel
Olshausenstraße 40, 24098 Kiel, Germany
{rub,fhu}@informatik.uni-kiel.de

Abstract

Many Computer Science curricula at universities start programming with a functional programming language (for instance, SML, Haskell, Scheme) and later change to the imperative programming paradigm. For the latter usually the object-oriented programming language Java is used. However, this puts a burden on the students, since even the smallest Java program cannot be formulated without the notion of class and static and public method. In this paper we present an approach for changing from functional to object-oriented programming. Using (Standard) ML for the functional programming paradigm, it still prepares the decisive notions of object-orientation by specific constructs of this language. As experience at the University of Kiel has shown, this smoothes the transition and helps the students getting started with programming in the Java language.

Categories and Subject Descriptors D.1.1 [*Applicative (functional) programming*]; D.1.5 [*Object-oriented programming*]; D.3.3 [*Language constructs and features*]

General Terms Languages

Keywords SML, signature, structure, functor, Java, object, class

1. Introduction

Many Computer Science curricula at universities start with the functional programming paradigm. This is mainly due to the fact that this paradigm cannot only be used to explain many basic concepts of programming and algorithm development, but also to teach a lot of fundamental concepts of Computer Science and how these concepts evolve from each other. A further advantage of functional programming is that it uses in the for novices very important initial stage only the notion of (recursive, partial) functions, which should be known from high school. Finally, it should be mentioned that functional programs allow to demonstrate proofs of simple program properties by combining structural or well-founded induction with equational reasoning.

Although functional programming has a lot of advantages, it is also important to familiarize students with imperative and object-oriented concepts already during the first year at the university. These concepts are widely used in industry and many topics of subsequent courses use imperative or object-oriented programming languages (especially, Java and C++). At the University of Kiel we change to imperative programming after the introduction to functional programming and use, as many other universities, the object-oriented programming language Java [2, 6]. However, experience has shown that this puts a burden on the students if one starts imperative programming with Java's overhead of object-oriented notations. Even the smallest Java program cannot be formulated without the notion of class and static and public (main) methods, and neglecting these notions at the beginning proved to be unsatisfactory for teachers as well as for students[1]. Therefore, we have decided to prepare the transition to Java already on the level of SML [8, 14], the language we use for the introduction to functional programming. Fortunately, this is possible due to the very rich module system and the reference mechanism of SML. As experience has shown, our approach smoothes the transition and helps students getting started with object-orientation and programming in Java.

The remainder of the paper is organized as follows. In Section 2 we outline the concept for the two first year courses in programming at the University of Kiel and describe our approach for changing from functional SML-programming to imperative/object-oriented Java-programming without going into details. Details of the approach are presented in the next three sections. Using a running example very similar to the well-known bank account example of the textbook [1], we show how to model objects, classes, and inheritance in SML and demonstrate the great similarity of the resulting pieces of SML-code and the corresponding Java-pieces. For these sections we assume the reader to be familiar with SML, including references and the module system, and with Java. In Section 6 we show the limitations of our approach and Section 7 contains some concluding remarks.

2. The Approach

At the University of Kiel, the two first year courses in programming are divided into "Programming" (first semester) and "Algorithms and Data Structures" (second semester). Both courses combine theoretical aspects of programming and algorithm development with practical aspects of these fields. In doing so, we want to avoid two disadvantages which frequently appear if one puts too much emphasis on one of these aspects. Overemphasizing practical programming may suggest to the students that theory has little to do with practice and they can become a good programmer

FDPE'05 September 25, 2005, Tallinn, Estonia.

[1] From a pedagogical point of view, there are many arguments against Java as first-course programming language at universities. We recommend the reader to have a look at [5].

without studying theory. On the other hand, overemphasizing theory may lead to the impression that theory as "mere theory" has its right (e.g., for studying the absolute or gradual limits of what algorithmically can be solved), but it is not relevant for programming practice.

Since more than one decade we use the functional paradigm in the first semester and the imperative paradigm in the second one. Due to certain reasons (e.g., its very clean implementation of most of the important object-oriented concepts and also to meet demands of industry), some years ago Java has been selected for the course on algorithms and data structures and it has been decided that the transition from the functional language to Java appears at the end of the first course. Giving the course on programming the first time and thereby starting with Java from the scratch, we noticed that such an approach puts a great burden on the students and the results did not meet our expectations. As a consequence, we decided to prepare the transition already on the level of SML. This was enabled by the following (rough) structure of the previous course on programming.

(1) Mathematical preliminaries (sets, logical notation, induction, terms, term replacement etc.).

(2) Introduction to functional programming (first-order recursive functions [10] over primitive types, parameter passing, unfold-fold technique etc.).

(3) Advanced concepts of functional programming (datatype declarations, recursive data types, pattern matching, higher-order functions, polymorphism, advanced programming techniques etc.).

(4) Data abstraction and modularization (information hiding, abstract types, signatures, structures, functors etc.).

(5) Introduction to Java (basic concepts of object-orientation, while-programs over primitive types, loop invariants, assertion technique for development etc.).

In the refined course, Part (4) is extended by a section which introduces and motivates object-orientation as a specific approach of modularization. Then descriptions of the fundamental notions *object*, *class*, and *inheritance* are given (*polymorphism* is discussed already in (3)). The main focus of this is to convey these notions in general and not as particular constructs of a programming language. To reach this aim, we proceed as follows:

- First objects are specified as "things" that have attributes and can perform actions.
- Then classes are introduced as descriptions of all objects (the *instances*) of a particular kind, together with the creation of instances.
- Finally, inheritance is explained as a mechanism that allows to derive new classes from given ones to deal with specific cases in adequate manner.

Having introduced these three notions, it is shown how they can be modeled within the known language SML by means of a suited example. Due to the great similarity of the resulting SML-code and a later formulation of the example in Java, this new approach smoothes the transition from SML to Java and avoids, as experience has shown, many teething troubles with the new language and paradigm. Of course, the extension of Part (4) required to shorten the other parts of the course a little bit and to move some topics into the second semester to stay within the time scheduled for one semester. This, however, caused no serious problems. A German version of the actual lecture notes on programming (winter semester 2004/05) is available via the Web [3].

3. Modeling Objects

Object-oriented programming is based on objects. As already mentioned in the last section, abstractly these are "things" that have attributes (also called fields) associated with it and that can perform certain actions. Attributes are ascertainable through their values. In object-oriented programming languages like Java they are specified by variables. Based on this, actions are performed by calls of methods which, in the most simple case, either compute values or change values of variables.

As an example, bank accounts can be considered as objects. In a very simple case (see [1]) the attributes of an account are given by the current account balance and the overdraft agreement. Two possible actions that compute values are the computation of the available money and the computation of the account balance. Attributes are changed, for example, by defining the new overdraft, by depositing and withdrawing money, and by deducing charges.

To model objects in SML, we use references instead of variables and functions instead of methods. Then an object corresponds to an SML-structure which consists of declarations of references for the attributes and of functions for the actions. Usually attributes (and auxiliary methods) of objects are declared to be private. Also this information hiding can be modeled in SML. We only have to define a SML-signature that exactly contains the names and types of the non-private (i.e., public) functions and after that to restrict structures through this signature.

In the case of our bank account example, the declaration of an object `A1` is described by the following SML-code. The two references `st` and `cr` in the structure declaration are used for the two attributes "account balance" and "overdraft"; the five functions realize the actions mentioned above. Hiding of `st` and `cr` is obtained by restricting the declared structure through an appropriate signature.

```
signature Account =
  sig
    val Available : unit -> int;
    val AccountBalance : unit -> int;
    val SetOverdraft : int -> unit;
    val Deposit : int -> unit;
    val Withdraw : int -> unit;
    val Charge : int -> unit;
  end;

structure A1 : Account =
  struct
    val st : int ref = ref 0;
    val cr : int ref = ref 0;

    fun Available () : int =
      !st + !cr;
    fun AccountBalance () : int =
      !st;
    fun SetOverdraft (n : int) : unit =
      cr := n;
    fun Deposit (n : int) : unit =
      st := !st + n;
    fun Withdraw (n : int) : unit =
      if n <= Available()
        then st := !st - n
        else ();
    fun Charge (n : int) : unit =
      st := !st - n;
  end;
```

As this example shows, we prefer to type SML-functions completely although the SML language possesses a sophisticated type inference mechanism. By adhering to this style, we hope to focus the student's attention on the importance of being aware of the arguments and results of each function one introduces in the course of a program. In the context of modeling object-orientation, furthermore, the result type `unit` indicates that a function/method changes values of attributes. It directly corresponds to the specification `void` in Java.

4. Modeling Classes

Abstractly, a class is a description of all objects of a particular kind, i.e., objects with the same attributes and actions. These objects are called instances. For each class there exists a mechanism for creating its instances.

Having a look at the bank account example of Section 3, one observes that the description of the account/object `A1` essentially is given by the right-hand side of the structure declaration, i.e., the code from `struct` to `end`. Creating a new account in the course of a program, say `A2`, therefore can be obtained by repeating the structure declaration by `A2` in lieu of `A1`. However, this is a laborious way of creating new objects. There exists a much more elegant way. It uses the functor mechanism of SML: an SML-functor operates on structures to produce other structures. Typically, the resulting structure is defined in the usual way, i.e., its constituents are parenthesized by the keywords `struct` and `end`, where in the declarations the constituents of the parameter structure may be used. From this point of view, functors are "parameterized" structures.

We have decided to model classes by functors, since functors frequently generalize structures in a way very similar to the generalization of objects to classes[2]. This approach enables us to model the generation of instances by simple functor calls which is possible due to the fact that SML-functors are not referentially transparent. If a functor is called with an argument twice, then the results of the calls are different structures.

In our bank account example, a parameterless functor modeling the class of accounts immediately arises from the above structure as follows:

```
functor new_Account () : Account =
  struct
    val st : int ref = ref 0;
    val cr : int ref = ref 0;

    fun Available () : int =
      !st + !cr;
    fun AccountBalance () : int =
      !st;
    fun SetOverdraft (n : int) : unit =
      cr := n;
    fun Deposit (n : int) : unit =
      st := !st + n;
    fun Withdraw (n : int) : unit =
      if n <= Available()
        then st := !st - n
        else ();
    fun Charge (n : int) : unit =
      st := !st - n;
  end;
```

Structurally, this SML-code is very similar to the code in Java, as the following Java-class `Account` for bank accounts shows:

```
class Account {
  private int st;
  private int cr;

  public int Available () {
    return st + cr; }
  public int AccountBalance () {
    return st; }
  public void SetOverdraft (int n) {
    cr = n; }
  public void Deposit (int n) {
    st = st + n; }
  public void Withdraw (int n) {
    if (n <= st + cr) st = st - n; }
  public void Charge (int n) {
    st = st - n;}
}
```

Using the above SML-functor `new_Account`, it is possible to generate accounts by structure declarations with simple functor calls as right-hand sides. A manipulation of instances then is possible by calls of the functions of the declared structures in statement lists, as the following simple example shows:

```
structure A1 : Account = new_Account();
A1.SetOverdraft(100);
A1.Deposit(100);
structure A2 : Account = new_Account();
A2.SetOverdraft(500);
A1.Withdraw(50);
```

We generate an account `A1`, put its overdraft to 100 units of money, and deposit 100 units of money. Then we generate a new account `A2` and put the overdraft of `A2` to 500 units of money. Finally, we withdraw 50 units of money from the first account `A1`.

Comparing this code with the following corresponding code in Java, the similarity becomes even more evident than in the case of classes; only the generation of the two instances syntactically differ.

```
Account A1 = new Account();
A1.SetOverdraft(100);
A1.Deposit(100);
Account A2 = new Account();
A2.SetOverdraft(500);
A1.Withdraw(50);
```

So far, we only considered parameterless functors. If we change to functors with parameters, then we are even able to model parameterized classes. This can be explained by our bank account example as well.

In the previous modeling of bank accounts the generation of a new account comes along with an overdraft agreement of 0 units of money. In practice, however, usually the opening of a new bank account is combined with a specific overdraft agreement. Taking the initialization of the overdraft as parameter, this can be modeled by a parameterized class. Then, instantiation means not only to create a new account but also to designate a particular value to its initial overdraft.

In SML a parameterization of a class can be modeled by a functor containing structures as parameters. In the case of the account example, name and type of the initial overdraft are specified by the signature of the parameter structure, for example, as follows:

```
signature Param =
  sig
    val o : int;
  end;
```

[2] In [14] SML-functors are even considered as a generalization of the idea of templates in C++, i.e., parameterized classes. We will descend to this at the end of Section 4.

The modeling functor itself is obtained from the previous functor new_Account by adding a parameter of signature Param, say P, and changing the initialization of cr from 0 to P.o. Hence, we have:

```
functor new_Account1 (P : Param) : Account =
  struct
    val st : int ref = ref 0;
    val cr : int ref = ref P.o;

    fun Available () : int =
      !st + !cr;
    fun AccountBalance () : int =
      !st;
    fun SetOverdraft (n : int) : unit =
      cr := n;
    fun Deposit (n : int) : unit =
      st := !st + n;
    fun Withdraw (n : int) : unit =
      if n <= Available() then st := !st - n
                          else ();
    fun Charge (n : int) : unit =
      st := !st - n;
  end;
```

If we call this functor, for example, with the anonymous structure

```
struct
  val o : int = 500;
end
```

as argument, then an instance is created with 500 as intital value of cr. In words this means that a new bank account is opened and this is combined with an overdraft agreement of 500 units of money.

It is obvious, how to change the signature Param and the functor new_Account1 to obtain besides an initial overdraft agreement also an initial deposit when opening a new bank account.

5. Modeling Inheritance

Having demonstrated how to model objects and classes in the language SML, it remains to show that this approach is appropriate for modeling inheritance as well. Inheritance is the third central concept of object-orientation and describes the deduction of new classes (the subclasses) from given ones (the superclasses) to deal with specific cases in adequate manner. We believe that inheritance is best explained to beginners by concrete examples which frequently occur in practice. Most of these examples are based on *specialization by inheritance*, that is the adaption of an existing general framework to a particular situation , since this is the central technique of object-orientation (see [11] for more details).

In the context of our running bank account example, a first kind of specialization is given by student accounts which are free of charge. For our SML model this means that we have to override the function Charge of the functor new_Account in such a way that a call of the new version does not collect charges, i.e., is without any effect. The result is the following functor:

```
functor new_StudAccount () : Account =
  struct
    structure A : Account = new_Account();
    open A;

    fun Charge (n : int) : unit =
      ();
  end;
```

In the structure specification forming the body of the functor new_StudAccount, we use a structure declaration in combination with the opening of the declared structure A via open A as a comfortable way to include the constituents of new_Account into the structure of new_StudAccount. Then the definition of Change from the structure A is overriden by a redefinition of the function. As the functor declaration shows, student accounts possess the same interface/signature as general bank accounts.

Another example of specialization by inheritance, which usually involves a modification of the signature, is to add specific functionality to a class. In this case it is sufficient just to add the new functionality. we will explain this again by means of our running examnple.

For bank accounts an additional functionality may be the possibility of online banking. In the most simple case this means to have an additional hidden Boolean attribute and an additional visible method with a truth value as argument such that a call of the method enables or disables online banking by changing the value of the hidden Boolean attribute accordingly. For our SML model this involves an extension of the signature Account by the name and functionality of the new method and an extension of the functor new_Account by its implementation, which uses a hidden reference declaration for implementing the new attribute. In the following SML-code the include-operation is used as a comfortable way to include the constituents of a signature in another one, and for the inclusion of constituents of a structure in an another structure again the open-operation is applied.

```
signature ExtAccount =
  sig
    include Account;
    val SetOnlinebanking : bool -> unit;
  end;

functor new_ExtAccount () : ExtAccount =
  struct
    structure A : Account = new_Account();
    open A;
    val ob : bool ref = ref false;

    fun SetOnlinebanking (b : bool) : unit =
      ob := b;
  end;
```

Because of the initialization of the reference ob by false, online banking is not possible for a newly opened bank account.

At this place it also should be remarked that a functor with a parameter of signature Account can be applied to a structure of the more general signature ExtAccount without previous conversion. We use this property of the ML module system to introduce the notion of *subtyping* to the students.

Here is the extension of the former Java-class Account to a subclass ExtAccount which models bank accounts with the possibility of online banking.

```
class ExtAccount extends Account {
  private bool ob;

  public void SetOnlinebanking (bool b) {
    ob = b;
  }
}
```

Since in Java the initial value of a Boolean variable is false, again online banking is not possible for a newly opened bank account.

Of course, from a purely syntactic point of view the Java-class ExtAccount is much more simple than the corresponding signature ExtAccount and functor new_ExtAccount in SML. However, structurally there is again a great similarity between the SML- and the Java-code for the extended of bank accounts, and exactly this is what we want to demonstrate.

6. Limitations of the Approach

In the preceeding sections we presented a way for changing from functional SML-programming to object-oriented Java-programming. It is especially tailored for beginners to make the transition as smooth as possible. Due to this aim, of course, the approach has its limitations and deficiencies if considered from a "mere object-oriented" point of view. These limitations will be discussed in the following.

The first limitation regards binding which we explain by an example. Consider the following situation. From the Java-class `Account` of Section 4 it is obvious to derive the following subclass `StudAccount` for student accounts which redefines the method `Charge` for deducing charges according to the former SML-model:

```
class StudAccount extends Account {
  public void Charge (int n) {
    ;}
}
```

Furthermore, let an instance `A` be generated. In Java then the class name used in the `new`-operator determines binding, i.e., which definition of the method name has to be used. A generation of `A` via

```
StudAccount A = new StudAccount();
```

implies that the method `A.Charge` is bound to the `Charge` of the subclass `StudAccount` if it is applied to an integer, whereas the assignment

```
StudAccount A = new Account();
```

implies that `A.Charge` is bound to the `Charge` of the superclass `Account`. In SML it is not easy to model this principle of *dynamic binding* which is the basis of the object-orientated variant of polymorphism. One needs structures as constituents of signatures and has carefully to follow the paths in the structures hierarchy.

We are also aware of the fact that our approach in some technical details is inaccurate if considered under theoretical aspects. For example, in object-oriented programming languages objects are values and not first-order only entities as signatures, structures, and functors in SML are.

Finally, we also know that we only introduce the core ideas of object-orientation and only show the students how the central concepts objects, classes, and inheritance can be modeled in SML. This also includes some small example programs but, of course, not a fundamental introduction into the development of programs in an object-oriented manner.

We do not regard these limitations and deficiencies as a disadvantage. Our approach never has been intended to be a detailed introduction in object-oriented analysis, design, and programming and further central concepts like frameworks or the well-known design patterns work orginating from [7]. This would be far beyond the possibilities of an introductionary course in programming. It is only supposed to smooth the transition from functional to object-oriented programming to help students of a first university course getting started with object-orientation and programming in Java. The second semester course on algorithms and data structures and subsequent specific lectures on software-engineering, object-orientation etc. together with their accompanying practical exercises then have to undertake the task of a detailed treatment of imperative and object-oriented programming in Java.

7. Conclusion

In this paper we have presented a new approach for a smooth transition from functional programming in SML to object-oriented programming in Java. It is especially designed for beginners in Computer Science at universities and has been tested at the University of Kiel in the winter semester 2004/05. We are highly pleased with the result. The preparation of object-orientation still in SML (and additional material in the lecture notes on the web) led to the fact that at the end of the semester most of the students had understood the basic principles of object-orientation and had been able to write (of course, not too large) Java programs. The proposed approach avoided many difficulties which appeared during an earlier course, where we started with Java from scratch. As a by-product, our approach leads to a deeper understanding of the module system of SML.

There exists an object-oriented ML-dialect, called OCaml [12]. Hence, the question arises: Why not start with OCaml instead of SML? Reasons for our use of SML are that it is the most popular member of the ML family, used in all well-established textbooks, and excellent public domain implementations exist. Furthermore, we want to place emphasis on modularization and encapsulation. This is adequately supported by the module system of SML. On the basis of the restricted time available for its treatment, we believe that our approach leads to a deeper understanding than a separation of modularization, encapsulation, and object-orientation using OCaml.

Our approach is based on special features of the SML programming language, especially its module system. Hence, the question arises whether it can be translated to other functional programming languages, especially Haskell [9, 4] and Scheme [1, 13]) which frequently are used for the introduction to functional programming at universities. We have not investigated this in great detail, but believe that in both cases the answer is "in principle 'yes', but ...". Concerning Haskell, we can use I/O-monads and `IORefs` to model attributes/variables and functions to change their values. Based on this, it seems to be possible to model objects and classes by functions, too. But we assume that the resulting model is rather complex and far beyond the possibilities of beginners. In contrast to Haskell, it is very easy to model attributes/variables and the change of their values in Scheme using the assignment-operation `!set` and the two special procedures `set-car!` and `set-cdr!`. But, to our best knowledge, in the standard of the language (as e.g., described in the language report [13]) there are no constructs for data abstraction and modularization. Hence, we believe that also Scheme is not appropriate for our approach.

Acknowledgement

We thank the referees for valuable remarks.

References

[1] Abelson H., Sussman G.J., Sussmann J.: Structure and interpretation of computer programs. MIT Press, 1999.

[2] Arnold K., Gosling J.: The Java programming language. Addison-Wesley, 1996.

[3] Berghammer R.: Informatik I (Programmierung). Lecture notes, University of Kiel, Inst. of Computer Science, available via URL www.informatik.uni-kiel.de/inf/Berghammer/teaching, 2005.

[4] Bird R.S.: Introduction to functional programming using Haskell. 2nd edition, Prentice Hall, 1998.

[5] Böszörmenye L.: Why Java is not my favorite first-course language. Software – Concepts & Tools 19, 141-145, 1998.

[6] Deitel H.M., Deitel P.J.: Java: How to program. 6th edition, Pearson Education International, 2005.

[7] Gamma E., Helm R., Johnson R., Vlissides J.: Design patterns: Elements of reusable object-oriented software. Addison Wesley, 1995.

[8] Harper R., Milner R., Tofte M.: The definition of Standard SML. MIT Press, 1991.

[9] Hudak P., Preyton-Jones S.L., Wadler P. (eds.): Report on the programming language Haskell. ACM SIGPLAN Notices 27(5), 1992.

[10] Loeckx J., Sieber K.: The foundations of program verification. Wiley, 1984.

[11] Poetzsch-Heffter A.: Konzepte objektorientierter Programmierung. Springer, 2000.

[12] Remy D., Vouillon J.: Objective ML: An effective object-oriented extension to ML. Theory and Practice of Object Systems 4 (1), 27-50 1998.

[13] Rees J., Clinger W. (eds.): The revised report on the algorithmic language Scheme. Lisp Pointers 4(3), 1991.

[14] Ullmann J.D.: Elements of ML programming, SML97 edition. Prentice Hall, 1998.

Laziness Without All the Hard Work

Combining Lazy and Strict Languages for Teaching

Eli Barzilay
Northeastern University
eli@barzilay.org

John Clements
Northeastern University
clements@brinckerhoff.org

Abstract

Students have trouble understanding the difference between lazy and strict programming. It is difficult to compare the two directly, because popular strict languages and popular lazy languages differ in their syntax, in their type systems, and in other ways unrelated to the lazy/strict evaluation discipline.

While teaching programming languages courses, we have discovered that an extension to PLT Scheme allows the system to accommodate both lazy and strict evaluation in the same system. Moreover, the extension is simple and transparent. Finally, the simple nature of the extension means that the resulting system provides a rich environment for both lazy and strict programs without modification.

Categories and Subject Descriptors D.3.m [*Programming Languages*]: Miscellaneous

General Terms Languages

Keywords Lazy and Eager Evaluation, Teaching Programming Languages, PLT Scheme

1. Introduction

Computer science professors all over the world recognize the significance of the definitional interpreter as a central tool in the understanding of programming languages. In this approach, students understand the similarities and differences between programming languages by writing interpreters for these languages. These interpreters are structurally similar to formal specifications of the languages they define (the *defined* languages). As the course progresses, the students learn about new programming language constructs by adding corresponding rules to their interpreters. Since each interpreter is an extension of the prior one, they are typically all written in the same *defining* language.

This approach is natural and informative, and it is adopted in one form or another by many modern programming languages textbooks [1, 8, 11]. In fact, this approach follows directly from the maxim that "the best way to learn is to teach" and the observation that writing a program is exactly this: the programmer must teach the computer how to perform the given task, in the most detailed and pedantic fashion imaginable.

FDPE'05 September 25, 2005, Tallinn, Estonia.

The notion of a definitional interpreter is an old one. Reynolds [12] provides a synopsis of earlier work and is the starting point for much of the later work. In this paper, Reynolds classifies definitional interpreters based on two key features of the defining language: whether they permit higher-order functions, and whether they are call-by-value or call-by-name.

This classification adds a second axis to the space of definitional interpreters. Along with the features we are adding to the defined language, we must also consider the set of features in the defining language. Do we wish to change them, as well?

At first glance, the answer is "no". After all, we have observed already that extending an interpreter is possible only when the new and old interpreters are written in the same language. Changing the defining language could force students to re-implement their interpreters and needlessly disorient them.

Turning again to the question of how students learn, however, we see that while they gain experience in specifying the defined language, their experience in *developing* programs lies only in the defining language. Indeed, students may graduate from such a course without having written more than a few two-line programs in each of the languages defined. That is, the only programs they write are the test cases for their interpreters.

The clearest example of this problem is in the difference between *strict* and *lazy* languages. In a strict language, arguments to a function are reduced to values before calling the function. In a lazy language, however, arguments to a function are evaluated only when they are needed. So, for instance, a function which does not use its first argument will not cause that argument to be evaluated. This change is sufficiently fundamental that most students understand laziness only after writing many programs in a lazy language. Merely altering an existing interpreter to define a lazy language may not be enough to internalize the difference between strict and lazy languages.

Some programming texts address this through what they call "horizonal" integration, rather than the "vertical" integration of extending a single interpreter with different features. Specifically, they supplement their definitional interpreters with small programming assignments in a language that contains the desired features. So, for instance, the students might practice writing programs in a lazy language such as Haskell before modifying their interpreters to behave lazily. The problem with this approach is that the key difference—laziness—is buried in an avalanche of other differences. Changes in syntax and changes in type systems prove to be very large obstacles, particularly for beginning programmers. Instead, we would like a language that can behave either lazily or strictly without changes to any other part of the system. That is, laziness should be orthogonal to other features of the language.

We have discovered that this is possible, using the PLT Scheme framework. By changing the "language level" to one that we provide, students may evaluate the same expressions in a strict language or in the corresponding lazy one. No changes whatsoever to the program text are required.

A combination of features makes this orthogonal switch possible. Scheme's syntax system [10] provides the tools needed to extend and alter the language, and PLT Scheme's module system provides the abstraction needed to make this change local, so that code written in the strict language is still evaluated eagerly.

A key advantage to this architecture is that PLT Scheme's existing facilities are available to both strict and lazy languages. This includes a rich set of libraries, and a variety of program tools, including a syntax checker, a coverage tester, and an error-tracing facility, among others [5, 3].

This paper has three more sections. In section 2, we show how the issue of laziness arises in a programming languages course, how our lazy language fits into the curriculum, and how the existing programming tools work without modification on the new language. In section 3, we show how the PLT scheme environment makes it possible to add laziness in a high-level way. Section 4 concludes.

2. Laziness in Action

To illustrate our extension, we consider a concrete example of its use. What follows is drawn from lectures given in Northeastern's Programming Languages course[1]. The course uses Krishnamurthi's textbook "Programming Languages: Application and Interpretation" [11]. In this approach, each new concept is

- introduced and analyzed in class,
- demonstrated in Scheme (the defining language),
- implemented as an extension of the defined language's interpreter,
- exercised at the defining level (usage) and the defined level (implementation).

Throughout the course, the students develop a series of interpreters whose complexity gradually increases.

Figure 1 shows the definition and the implementation of a simple language[2] that is demonstrated in the early stages of the course. Since the students have experience only with eager languages, they read this interpreter as the definition of an eager language, and they translate this belief to the formal definition as well.

This provides a natural entry for a discussion of lazy evaluation, and to explain that the evaluation rules for 'with' and for 'call' can be modified to operate in a lazy way,[3] which will change the defined language to a lazy one:

$$\text{eval}(\{\text{with}\ \{x\ E_1\}\ E_2\}) \ \longrightarrow\ \text{eval}(E_2[E_1/x])$$
$$\text{eval}(\{\text{call}\}\ E_1\ E_1) \ \longrightarrow\ \text{eval}(E_f[E_2/x])\ \text{ if} \ldots$$

However, going back to the (apparently) eager version that was defined and implemented, we can see (as noted by Reynolds) that the defined language is eager only because our defining language is eager, and that in fact the formal definition is non-deterministic in this regard. Students have difficulty understanding this possibility, and assume that the definition given could only be that of a strict language.[4]

One possible approach is to make a quick detour and introduce Haskell [9] — a language that is considerably different from Scheme in both syntax and semantics. As mentioned above, we believe that this approach puts an additional burden on students, since Haskell differ from Scheme on many fronts on top of its choice of evaluation order. For a crowd of stronger students, this might work, but we believe that for the average student, the simultaneous changes may be distracting.

2.1 Our Solution: A Lazy Scheme

Before settling on a solution, we considered and discarded several alternative approaches, including the following:

- Implement an interpreter which students use as their defining language. This leads to a heavy performance hit, making it impossible for students to run anything more than toy programs in their interpreter.
- Have the students implement a lazy language, and then assign exercises to be implemented in their defined language. The main problem here is that students consider their defined language as a toy, so they will dismiss such exercises as no more than mere academic illustrations, and by association dismiss lazy evaluation as such.
- Avoid introducing a lazy language, and instead demonstrate some restricted laziness in the defining language. For example, use Scheme's 'delay' and 'force' to demonstrate some degree of laziness. While practical, the explicit nature of the abstraction prevents a deep understanding of the differences between lazy and eager evaluation.

We believe that actual programming experience is crucial for internalizing lazy programming. Switching languages makes it less accessible, and the above approaches avoid making students experience lazy programming first-hand.

In short, we need a practical implementation of a lazy variant of Scheme, which should be implemented as an extension of our existing language. As we shall see in the following section, there are several features that are unique to PLT Scheme which make it possible to define a "new language" with different semantics, yet have it be a well-behaved part of the same system. This means that we get the environment support of DrScheme, as well as functionality that exists in many libraries that are included in PLT Scheme. The lazy language is implemented as a module, so existing code that does not use this module is not affected. It is also possible to use standard code from a lazy program and vice versa, under certain conditions — procedures from normal Scheme modules are treated as strict primitives in lazy code, and values from lazy modules can contain delayed promises in strict code.

2.2 Examples

The Lazy Scheme language is bundled as a PLT package that is used in the course. (The interested reader can install it from `http://csu660.barzilay.org/csu660.plt`[5].) Once the package is installed, DrScheme's language selection dialog will have a new "CSU660 Lazy Scheme" entry which makes the definitions and interactions windows use the lazy language.

As a first example, we can enter some code and witness how only the parts that are required by interaction output is executed. By default, the Lazy Scheme language level uses DrScheme's syntactic coverage feature, which highlights code that is "touched" during evaluation. Figure 2 shows a DrScheme screenshot that demonstrates such an interaction[6].

As this demonstrates, constructors of lists ('cons', 'list', 'list*') and of other objects are properly lazy in the new language, and accessors are strict. This means that instead of dealing

[1] CSU660, `http://www.ccs.neu.edu/course/csu660/`

[2] This is Krishnamurthi's 'FWAE' language. Curly braces are used in defined languages to avoid confusing them with the defining language.

[3] A little later in the course we discuss name capturing.

[4] We imagine that students learning in Haskell would be similarly impaired, although in the other direction.

[5] Currently, this requires using version 209 of PLT Scheme.

[6] Coverage is indicated by colors, underlines added here for printout clarity.

$$\text{eval}(N) \rightarrow N$$

$$\text{eval}(\{+\ E_1\ E_2\}) \rightarrow \text{eval}(E_1) + \text{eval}(E_2)$$

$$\text{eval}(\{-\ E_1\ E_2\}) \rightarrow \text{eval}(E_1) - \text{eval}(E_2)$$

$$\text{eval}(\{*\ E_1\ E_2\}) \rightarrow \text{eval}(E_1) * \text{eval}(E_2)$$

$$\text{eval}(Id) \rightarrow \text{error}$$

$$\text{eval}(\{\text{with}\ \{x\ E_1\}\ E_2\}) \rightarrow \text{eval}(E_2[\text{eval}(E_1)/x])$$

$$\text{eval}(F) \rightarrow F \quad \text{(for a function expression } F\text{)}$$

$$\begin{aligned}&\text{eval}(\{\text{call}\}\ E_1\ E_1)\\ &\rightarrow \text{eval}(E_f[\text{eval}(E_2)/x]) \ \text{if eval}(E_1) = \{\text{fun}\{x\}E_f\}\\ &\rightarrow \text{error} \quad \text{otherwise}\end{aligned}$$

$\Longrightarrow$

```
;; eval : FWAE -> FWAE
;; Evaluates FWAE expressions by reducing them
;; to value expressions.
(define (eval expr)
  (cases expr
    [(Num n) expr]
    [(Add l r) (fwae-add (eval l) (eval r))]
    [(Sub l r) (fwae-sub (eval l) (eval r))]
    [(Mul l r) (fwae-mul (eval l) (eval r))]
    [(With bound-id named-expr bound-body)
     (eval (subst bound-body
                  bound-id
                  (Num (eval named-expr))))]
    [(Id v) (error 'eval "free identifier: ~s" v)]
    [(Fun bound-id bound-body) expr]
    [(Call (Fun bound-id bound-body) arg-expr)
     (eval (subst bound-body
                  bound-id
                  (eval arg-expr)))]
    [(Call something arg-expr)
     (error 'eval
            "expected a function, got: ~s"
            something)]))
```

Figure 1. Definition and implementation of a simple language

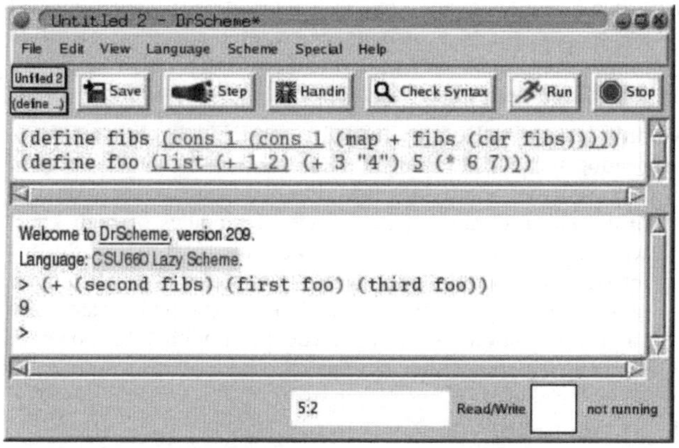

Figure 2. Demonstrating syntactic coverage in Lazy Scheme

```
(define nats (cons 1 (map add1 nats)))
(define (divides? n m)
  (zero? (modulo m n)))
(define (sift n l)
  (filter (lambda (x) (not (divides? n x))) l))
(define (sieve l)
  (cons (car l) (sieve (sift (car l) (cdr l)))))
(define (n-primes n) (take n (sieve (cdr nats))))
```

Figure 3. Using infinite lists in lazy Scheme

with special names for operations on streams [1, 2], we use known Scheme names: the language is the same, only the evaluation order changed. The code in Figure 3 demonstrates using infinite lists in plain Scheme syntax.

Finally, we can get back to Reynolds' observation, which is demonstrated effectively using our Lazy Scheme. Almost any of the interpreters that are implemented throughout the course, e.g., the code in Figure 1, can be used *as is* in the Lazy Scheme context to yield a lazy evaluator. Re-examining the code in Figure 1, reveals that there is a little more than plain Scheme to our interpreter. The '`cases`' expression is a syntactic extension that is used throughout the course, together with a new '`define-type`' declaration. '`define-type`' is used to define a type which is a disjoint union of a few record variants, and '`cases`' checks the type of its input and deconstruct it by pattern-matching. Together, they are roughly equivalent to using types in a statically typed (functional) language like ML. This functionality is implemented by some non-trivial syntactic code. It is essential to the coursework, so it must be present in the Lazy Scheme language as well; which is easily achieved by using the *same code* in the two contexts. This confirms the usability of the lazy language, since it is used with code that implement our teaching framework.

Figure 4 shows a more sophisticated evaluator. Once again, this code is valid in both languages, yielding an eager or a lazy evaluator.

3. Implementing a Lazy Scheme

Our lazy language implementation relies heavily on PLT Scheme's module system [7]. This system provides a robust way of defining modules that export both standard functionality and syntax transformations. The core of the lazy language delays all function applications, and forces arguments to strict functions — this is a known solution to the off-by-one problem that naive stream implementations suffer from (our solution is similar to even-style streams [13]). This is implemented by the following transformation:

```
(f x ...)
  -> (~ (let ([f (! f)])
          (if (lazy? f) (f x ...) (f (! x) ...))))
```

where '$\sim$' is '`delay`' and '`!`' is '`force`' iterated as many times as necessary to get a value. The rationale behind iterating '`force`' is that we avoid complex bookkeeping (e.g., SRFI-40 [2]) by treating all promises as delayed expressions. Actually, the Scheme Report mentions treating promises as the values they encapsulate as a viable implementation strategy [10, Section 6.4]: "It may be the case that there is no means by which a promise can be operationally distinguished from its forced value".

The principle is therefore simple; PLT Scheme has a combination of powerful features that makes it possible to implement this lazy language in a way that cooperates with the environment, so that strict and lazy code can be combined via the module system.

```
(define-type FLANG
  [Num  (n number?)]
  [Add  (lhs FLANG?) (rhs FLANG?)]
  [Sub  (lhs FLANG?) (rhs FLANG?)]
  [Mul  (lhs FLANG?) (rhs FLANG?)]
  [Div  (lhs FLANG?) (rhs FLANG?)]
  [Id   (name symbol?)]
  [With (name symbol?) (named FLANG?) (body FLANG?)]
  [Fun  (name symbol?) (body FLANG?)]
  [Call (fun-expr FLANG?) (arg-expr FLANG?)])

;; eval : FLANG env -> VAL
;; evaluates FLANG expressions by reducing them to values
(define (eval expr env)
  (cases expr
    [(Num n) (NumV n)]
    [(Add l r) (arith-op + (eval l env) (eval r env))]
    [(Sub l r) (arith-op - (eval l env) (eval r env))]
    [(Mul l r) (arith-op * (eval l env) (eval r env))]
    [(Div l r) (arith-op / (eval l env) (eval r env))]
    [(With bound-id named-expr bound-body)
     (eval bound-body
           (Extend bound-id (eval named-expr env) env))]
    [(Id v) (lookup v env)]
    [(Fun bound-id bound-body)
     (FunV (lambda (arg-val)
             (eval bound-body
                   (Extend bound-id arg-val env))))]
    [(Call fun-expr arg-expr)
     (let ([fval (eval fun-expr env)])
       (cases fval
         [(FunV proc) (proc (eval arg-expr env))]
         [else (error 'eval
                      "expected a function, got: ~s"
                      fval)]))]))
```

Figure 4. Parts of an evaluator code that can be used *as is* in both strict and lazy Scheme

The following is a list of these features and how they contribute to the implementation. The MzScheme language manual [6] describes these features in detail.

Primitive application syntax: The transformation that we use is needed for all function application forms. In most Scheme implementations, this requires implementing a code-walker that can identify and ignore special forms and macros and is able to deal with code that is generated by macros.

In PLT Scheme, however, all function applications are first expanded as uses of the special '`#%app`' syntax [6, Section 12.5]. Furthermore, it is possible to create a new 'language module' that can provide its own version of Scheme primitives, including the '`#%app`' syntax. Our lazy language module uses this to implement the transformation of application forms. Figure 5 shows the relevant part of the (simplified) code that implements the new '`#%app`' as well as a new '`apply`' function (the '`provide`' form is in charge of exporting a '`mzscheme`'-like language, except for new versions of '`#%app`' and '`apply`').

Note also that '`!`' is a function in the strict implementation, but it must be treated as a special form when it is used in the resulting lazy language or it will get delayed like other functions — strictness in a lazy language must be a special form [4].

Applicable records: For the implementation of our transformation we need to determine when a function is lazy. Obviously, known built-in constructors like '`cons`' and '`list`' are lazy, and non-constructor primitives are strict. But we cannot assume that all non-built-in functions are lazy or we would not be able to use Scheme functions from conventional modules imported as strict functionality.

The solution exercises PLT Scheme's ability to define new record types ('structs') that can be applied as functions. This

```
(module lazy mzscheme
  (define-syntax (~app stx)
    (syntax-case stx (!)
      ;; do not treat this as normal applications
      [(_ ! x) (syntax/loc stx (! x))]
      [(_ f x ...)
       (with-syntax
           ([(y ...) (generate-temporaries #'(x ...))])
         (~ (let ([p (! f)] [y x] ...)
              (if (lazy? p) (p y ...) (p (! y) ...)))))]))
  (define (~apply f . xs)
    (let ([f (! f)] [xs (!list (apply list* xs))])
      (apply f (if (lazy? f) xs (map ! xs)))))
  (provide (all-from-except mzscheme #%app apply)
           (rename ~app #%app)
           (rename ~apply apply)))
```

Figure 5. Implementing lazy function applications

can be used to annotate function values with source code, documentation, etc. We redefine '`lambda`' so it generates such tagged functions, making it possible to know when a function value was generated by lazy code. Checking for lazy functions is now simple: those that are tagged as lazy cover user-defined code and built-in constructors (which are re-provided as tagged values), record constructors are also considered lazy. All other functions are strict.

Technicalities: There are a few user-interaction technicalities that are specific for PLT Scheme. For example, setting a custom printer that forces (nested) evaluation results rather than have users force values they want to see.

Module system and syntax transformers: Finally, it is worth repeating that the resulting module cooperates with the rest of PLT Scheme — bindings from the two languages are not confused, and programs can be made of modules of both kinds without problems; many DrScheme tools "just work". Specifically, separate compilation works as expected even when modules are developed separately and later combined as parts of a single application. This is a good demonstration of the power of the PLT Scheme module system [7].

4. Conclusion

Our work demonstrates two things. First, that PLT Scheme's syntax and module systems make it possible to add such fundamental features as laziness to an existing language in a transparent and high-level way. Second, that such an extension has the crucial advantage that it inherits a wealth of libraries and environment tools.

As a result of these developments, it is now possible to show students in a programming languages course the difference between strict and lazy languages in isolation. That is, students can compare strict and lazy evaluations of the same program text. Furthermore, they can do so without giving up existing libraries, or their current set of tools.

References

[1] H. Abelson, G. J. Sussman, and J. Sussman. *Structure and Interpretation of Computer Programs*. MIT Press, Cambridge, MA, 1985.

[2] P. L. Bewig. SRFI 40: A library of streams. `http://srfi.schemers.org/srfi-40/`.

[3] J. Clements, M. Felleisen, R. Findler, M. Flatt, and S. Krishnamurthi. Fostering little languages. *Dr. Dobb's Journal*, March 2004. (Invited Paper).

[4] M. Felleisen. On the expressive power of programming languages. *Science of Computer Programming*, 17:35–75, 1991.

[5] R. B. Findler, J. Clements, C. Flanagan, M. Flatt, S. Krishnamurthi, P. Steckler, and M. Felleisen. Drscheme: A programming environment for Scheme. *Journal of Functional Programming*, 2001.

[6] M. Flatt. PLT MzScheme: Language manual. `http://www.plt-scheme.org/software/`, 1996–2005.

[7] M. Flatt. Composable and compilable macros: You want it *when?* In *ACM SIGPLAN International Conference on Functional Programming*, 2002.

[8] D. P. Friedman, M. Wand, and C. T. Haynes. *Essentials of Programming Languages*. MIT Press, Cambridge, MA, 2nd edition, 2001.

[9] P. Hudak and P. Wadler. Report on the programming language Haskell. Technical Report YALE/DCS/RR777, Yale University, Department of Computer Science, August 1991.

[10] R. Kelsey, W. Clinger, and J. Rees (Eds.). Revised^5 report of the algorithmic language Scheme. *ACM SIGPLAN Notices*, 33(9):26–76, 1998.

[11] S. Krishnamurthi. Programming languages: Application and interpretation. `www.cs.brown.edu/~sk/Publications/Books/ProgLangs/`, 2003–2005.

[12] J. C. Reynolds. Definitional interpreters for higher-order programming languages. In *ACM '72: Proceedings of the ACM annual conference*, pages 717–740. ACM Press, 1972.

[13] P. Wadler, W. Taha, and D. MacQueen. How to add laziness to a strict language, without even being odd. In *Workshop on Standard ML*, Baltimore, September 1998.

Word Puzzles in Haskell

Interactive Games for Functional Programming Exercises

S.A. Curtis

Oxford Brookes University

sharoncurtis@brookes.ac.uk

Abstract

This paper describes some functional programming exercises in the form of implementing some interactive word puzzle games. The games share a common framework and provide good opportunities for practising higher-order functions, recursion, and other list processing functions. Experience suggests that these games are motivating and enjoyable for students.

Categories and Subject Descriptors D.1.1 [*Programming Techniques*]: Applicative (Functional) Programming; K.3.2 [*Computers and Education*]: Computer and Information Science Education

General Terms Haskell, word puzzles, programming exercises

Keywords functional programming, education, assessment

1. Introduction

When setting functional programming exercises for students, it is a challenge to set exercises that meet certain criteria: as well as their suitability for learning the desired concepts, the activities should be easily explainable, students should be able to see useful applications of functional programming, the tasks should offer a range of difficulty suited to the range of the students, and the exercises should be enjoyable and motivating. Several authors including Aerts and De Vlaminck [1] and Lüth [4] have made the point that functional programming exercises using games are fun and motivating. Lüth [4] and Hudak [3] have also demonstrated that use of graphics interests and motivates students.

We suggest that text-based word puzzle games can also provide a fun interesting way for students to learn about functional programming, and can showcase the use of standard concepts for list processing, such as higher-order functions, recursion and list comprehensions. This paper describes a interactive loop useful for word puzzle games, along with two word puzzles; these were used for exercises for an introductory undergraduate functional programming course. Other teachers of functional programming may find these word puzzle games useful, either as is, or as inspiration. These exercises are implemented in Haskell, but they could be adapted for use with other functional languages.

FDPE'05 September 25, 2005, Tallinn, Estonia.

2. Interactive Games

The word puzzle games allow a single human player to try and solve a puzzle presented by the computer. These text-based games run in an interactive loop, such that at each step, the player types in an input string, and the computer displays a response, which typically shows the current state of the game. The game ends when either the puzzle is solved, the player runs out of guesses, or the player types the string `"quit"`.

At the heart of the implementation of the word puzzle games is a function to change the state of the game. Using a datatype `State`, the programming exercises given to students mainly involved the writing of such a state-changing function `scfn`:

```
scfn :: State -> String -> (String,State)
```

Thus `scfn` takes the previous state and the player's input string and returns a pair consisting of a string to be displayed on screen, and the new state. The displayed string could be, for example, a display showing the new state of the game, or an error message, or some kind of help message. Students also had to implement the function

```
displaySt :: State -> String
```

to produce a string for displaying the current state of the game, or rather, displaying only the information about the state that the puzzle player is permitted to know!

The code involving IO for both word puzzle games was supplied to the students. This included the function `game`, which provides the framework for both games:

```
game :: (State -> String -> (String,State))
        -> State -> String -> String -> IO ()
game scfn init prompt title =
   interact (untilEnd .
            (writeStr intro
             $ session scfn init prompt))
      where intro = "\n" ++ title ++
                    "\n(\"quit\" to quit)\n\n"
                    ++ displaySt init
```

Thus a particular word puzzle game can be specified from a state-changing function (`scfn`), an initial state (`init`), along with prompt and title strings. The function `interact` (from the module `Interact`) is used to provide the interactive loop for the game.

The remainder of the IO code for the word puzzle games is listed in the appendix.

3. The Wordguess Puzzle

This game is a simplified version of the traditional game *Hangman*: the computer chooses a word secretly and displays how many letters are in the word, and players attempt to guess the whole word by guessing individual letters. As letters are guessed correctly, their positions in the word are revealed. If a player guesses too many incorrect letters, the game is lost. Here is an extract of a sample run of the WordGuess game:

```
*** WordGuess ***
("quit" to quit)

        - - - - - - -

Not guessed yet: abcdefghijklmnopqrstuvwxyz
Lives left: 5
Please guess a letter: e
 ** Character not in word **

        - - - - - - -

Not guessed yet: abcd fghijklmnopqrstuvwxyz
Lives left: 4
Please guess a letter: a

        _ _ _ a _ _ _

Not guessed yet:  bcd fghijklmnopqrstuvwxyz
Lives left: 4
Please guess a letter:
```

(...several guesses later...)

```
        t o _ a r d s

Not guessed yet:  bc  fg ijklmn pq   uvwx z
Lives left: 2
Please guess a letter: w

        t o w a r d s

Not guessed yet:  bc  fg ijklmn pq   uv x z
Lives left: 2
 ** Well done, you got it! **
```

The state of the game can be captured in a triple containing the hidden word, the number of lives the player has left (the number of lives left is equal to the number of incorrect guesses it takes to lose the game), and a list of characters that have been guessed so far:

```
type State = (HiddenWord,LivesLeft,Guessed)

type HiddenWord = String
type LivesLeft = Int
type Guessed = [Char]
```

The WordGuess game can then be defined:

```
wordGuess seed = game makeAGuess init prompt title
  where which  = (randomNum seed)
                   `mod` (length wordList)
        word   = wordList !! which
        init   = (word,5,"")
        prompt = "Please guess a letter: "
        title  = "*** WordGuess ***"
```

The game is run from a command such as `wordGuess 35`. The number (e.g. 35) is chosen by the player to provide the seed for the function `randomNum` (supplied to students) which generates a suitable random number to select a hidden word out of the word list `wordList`. This list was prepared from a list of 1000 common English words (a sizable proportion of the students were non-native English speakers, so very well-known words were more suitable), filtered to exclude words with non-alphabetic characters, and words that were too short.

Maybe the simple challenge of implementing the functions `makeAGuess` (to change the game's state) and `displaySt` (to display the game's state) would be a suitably challenging specification for some groups of students. For this particular group of students, however, more help was given, with parts of `makeAGuess` implemented for them. The students' tasks were to implement a variety of interesting string-processing functions, of varying difficulty.

For example, one function the students were asked to write was a function `wordDisplay`, which displays the word that the player is trying to guess, with already-guessed letters displayed in their correct places, and not-yet-guessed letters displayed as underscores. This offered a good opportunity to use a map:

```
wordDisplay :: HiddenWord -> Guessed -> String
wordDisplay wd guesses
       = "         " ++
         concat (map (hideLetters guesses) wd)

hideLetters :: String -> Char -> String
hideLetters guesses c
    | elem c guesses  = [c,' ']
    | otherwise        = "_ "
```

Another task was to test whether the player had successfully completed the puzzle. This task afforded more opportunities to experiment with higher order functions and/or recursion, and a few students managed a neat definition using a list comprehension:

```
ended :: HiddenWord -> Guessed -> Bool
ended wd guessed = and [ elem c guessed | c <- wd]
```

4. The Cryptogram Puzzle

In this traditional puzzle, the computer chooses a text and a simple *substitution cipher*, which is a matching between `[1..26]` and `['a'..'z']`. The structure of the text is displayed along with the number encodings, and the player keeps guessing which number encodes which letter, until the whole text is revealed correctly. Here is an extract from a sample run of the game:

```
*** Cryptogram ***
("quit" to quit)


 _  _  _  _      _  _  _      _  _  _  _
 17 7  26 3      20 16 23     17 7  23 3
 _  _  _  _      _  _  _      _  _        _  _  _ .
 22 20 7  17     18 9  5      16 9        26 20 16

Guess a number=letter: 3=e
          e                            e
 _  _  _  _      _  _  _      _  _  _  _
 17 7  26 3      20 16 23     17 7  23 3
 _  _  _  _      _  _  _      _  _        _  _  _ .
 22 20 7  17     18 9  5      16 9        26 20 16
```

(...several guesses later...)

```
Guess a number=letter: 16=d
 t  i  _  e      a  d  _      t  i  _  e
 17 7  26 3      20 16 23     17 7  23 3
 w  a  i  t      _  _  _      d  _        _  a  d .
 22 20 7  17     18 9  5      16 9        26 20 16

Guess a number=letter: n=16
I didn't understand "n=16"
Try again! (sample usage: 5=h )

Guess a number=letter: 16=n
 t  i  _  e      a  n  _      t  i  _  e
 17 7  26 3      20 16 23     17 7  23 3
```

```
w  a  i  t     _  _  _     n  _      _  a  n .
22 20 7  17    18 9  5     16 9      26 20 16
```

(...several guesses later...)

```
t  i  m  e     a  n  d     t  i  d  e
17 7  26 3     20 16 23    17 7  23 3
w  a  i  t     f  o  _     n  o      m  a  n .
22 20 7  17    18 9  5     16 9      26 20 16
```

```
Guess a number=letter: 5=r
*** Well done! ***
Time and tide
wait for no man
 -- Unknown
```

The state information that needs to be kept in this word puzzle consists of three things: a quotation, the encryption that was chosen to encrypt it, and the player's current guesses:

```
type State = (Quotation,Encryption,PairsGuessed)

type Quotation = (String,String)
type Encryption = [(Int,Char)]
type PairsGuessed = [(Int,Char)]
```

A quotation consists of a pair of strings: the quotation itself, and the author of the quotation. The text may contain newline and other non-alphabetic characters. An encryption is a list of pairs, of numbers (from 1 to 26) and characters, and so is the list of the player's current guesses. These lists all use lower-case letters, and contain no duplicates or inconsistencies, although the guesses that the player currently holds about the encryption may or may not be correct.

The Cryptogram game is then defined:

```
cryptogram seed = game codeGuess init prompt title
  where init   = generateInitialState seed
        prompt = "Guess a number=letter: "
        title  = "*** Cryptogram ***"
```

where `generateInitialState` is the function that randomly chooses the initial text and encryption. The texts are chosen from a prepared list of short well-known quotations, and like the WordGuess puzzle, a seed number supplied by the player of the game is used for the randomization.

In the Cryptogram game, student challenges involved the implementation of the state-changing function `codeGuess` and the displaying of the current state of the game, similar to the WordGuess game, and again, some of the implementation was given to students, leaving the students specific tasks to complete the game.

The functional programming concepts involved in the tasks were varied: the production of the encryption offered an opportunity to experiment with the common library function `zip`, whilst the display involved plenty of use of `map` and `concat` functions. A variety of list processing functions were useful: `findChar` and `findInt` functions involved looking up characters and integers in encryption or guess lists, and updating the list of guesses proved a good discriminator between students as they had to bear in mind that a new `(number,letter)` guess might have to replace both a previous guess with that number and a previous guess with that letter:

```
updateGuesses :: (Int,Char) -> [(Int,Char)]
                  -> [(Int,Char)]
updateGuesses (i,c) xs =
        (i,c) : [(j,d) | (j,d) <- xs, j/=i, d/=c]
```

Parsing the input string to extract the letter and number, including error handling, produced a a variety of creative attempts from students. Also, like the WordPuzzle game, testing the current state to see whether the game has ended or not proved to be a good challenge. Students had to think carefully as they had to realise that only letters in the quotation should be tested, as a player can't reasonably be expected to guess the codes for letters that are not in the quotation:

```
cryptoGuessed :: State -> Bool
cryptoGuessed ((q,a),codes,ps)
    = and [ (correctCode (toLowerCase c) codes ps)
          | c <- q, isLetter c]

correctCode :: Char -> Encryption
            -> PairsGuessed -> Bool
correctCode c codes ps =
     c==(findChar (findInt c codes) ps)
```

5. Discussion

The general reaction from students was that they had enjoyed this piece of assessed work, which was singled out for particular praise in the end-of-course feedback. The choice of word puzzles for a group including many international students did not turn out to be a problem, though one student (a non-native English speaker) said that he found playing the games themselves to be a bit difficult, and he better enjoyed the challenge of programming the games. Either way, motivation displayed by students was high. Many students gained good marks, and displayed a lot of creativity and determination in their attempts to produce the required functions. From the teacher's point of view, several lessons were learnt from setting these exercises:

1. Giving plenty of examples helped to clarify to students what they were being asked to do.
2. Providing sample test data for lengthy input (e.g. the encryptions) was also useful in encouraging students to test their functions.
3. If the formatting of an output string needs to be precise (e.g. letters separated by a particular number of spaces) then this must be precisely specified.
4. Similarly, as the formatting of strings may need to be precise, care also has to be taken over the formatting of instructions. For these exercises, the instructions were presented in HTML, and browsers had no compunction about altering carefully-specified spacing, for example by inserting a newline character to produce a misleading or confusing effect.
5. Instructions should be explicit about what datatype invariants can and cannot be assumed. For example, if it can safely be assumed that a letter is lower case, or a particular list is not ordered, then this should be mentioned.

The word puzzles offered plenty of scope for students to try out a wide variety of functional programming techniques, and students could see the roles of the various functions within the word puzzle games, so the relevance and purpose was clear. The overall idea of the word puzzle games allowed the setting of exercises offering a variety of challenges, from simple uses of library functions up to complex uses of higher-order functions, and even the use of monads. The exercises provided a good differentiator, whilst allowing all students to show something of what they could do.

In the future, the intention is to reuse the same interactive game framework with different word puzzle games (to prevent answers being recycled), or even extend it to other text-based interactive games. Lessons learnt from these exercises provide inspiration to help students to learn more about identifying invariants and programming with them.

It is hoped these ideas may serve as inspiration for other teachers of functional languages. More details about these word puzzle game exercises can be found at [2].

A. Appendix

The termination of the interactive loop of the game is achieved by matching lines of output against a specific string:

```
untilEnd :: String -> String
untilEnd = unlines
           . (takeWhile (not . gameOver))
           . lines

gameOver :: String -> Bool
gameOver str = (str == gameEndString)

gameEndString = "Bye."
```

These functions are used in the loop for the interactive game, and include built-in testing for an early game termination request from the player:

```
session :: (State -> String -> (String,State))
          -> State -> String -> String -> String
session scfn st prompt
       = readLine prompt (\inStr ->
         let (str,st') = nextState scfn st inStr
         in writeStr (str ++ "\n\n")
            $ session scfn st' prompt)


nextState :: (State -> String -> (String, State))
            -> State -> String -> (String, State)
nextState scfn st inStr
  | inStr == "quit" = (gameEndString ++ "\n\n",st)
  | otherwise         = scfn st inStr
```

References

[1] K. Aerts and K. D. Vlaminck. Games provide fun(ctional programming tasks). In *Proceedings of the Workshop on Functional and Declarative Programming in Education*. ICFP, September 1999.

[2] S. Curtis. Word puzzles in Haskell. `http://cms.brookes.ac.uk/staff/SharonCurtis/teaching/archives/fp/wordpuzzles/`, 2005.

[3] P. Hudak. *The Haskell School of Expression: Learning Functional Programming Through Multimedia*. Cambridge University Press, 2000.

[4] C. Lüth. Haskell in space. *Journal of Functional Programming*, 13(6):1077–1085, November 2003.

Teaching of Image Synthesis in Functional Style

Jerzy Karczmarczuk

Dept. d'Informatique, Université de Caen, France

karczma@info.unicaen.fr

Abstract

We have taught the 3D modelling and image synthesis for computer science students (Master level), exploiting very intensely the functional *style* of programming/scene description. Although no pure functional language was used, since we wanted to use popular programmable packages, such as POV-Ray, or the interactive modeller/renderer Blender, scriptable in Python, we succeded in showing that typical functional tools, such as higher-order functional objects, compositions and recursive combinations are useful, easy to grasp and to implement. We constructed implicit and parametric surfaces in a generic way, we have shown how to transform (deform) and blend surfaces using functional methods, and we have even found a case where the laziness, implemented through Python generators, turned to be useful.

We exploited also some functional methods for the image processing: creation of procedural textures and their transformation.

Categories and Subject Descriptors D [*1*]: 1

General Terms Algorithms, Design, Languages

Keywords Image synthesis, Functional style

1. Introduction

The teaching of functional programming *techniques* at the University level falls sometimes into a methodological trap: the FP is *separated* from the rest of the curriculum; we often teach functional languages and tools during the first two years, with plenty of pedagogical examples, and then our students discover that the algorithms and practical exercices usually implemented in other languages have not too much in common with the initial pedagogical approaches, since when the research domains of teachers are far from FP, their teaching methodologies are different as well; later on, the teaching of compilation, of artificial intelligence techniques, etc. is often far from functional methods...

We have attempted, for several years, to exploit a different strategy, more integrated with other domains we taught, where functional tools were simply ... tools, used in specific contexts, without raising the question of their suitability in general, but following the idea that if our students learnt some functional techniques/style, they should apply them.

FDPE'05 September 25, 2005, Tallinn, Estonia.

- We used functional tools in compilation (not only classical parsing tools, but the construction of functional virtual machines [1], and typing); the full course was based on Haskell.
- The teaching of the 'scientific programming'(using various languages) exploited streams for solutions of differential equations, signals and random generators, insisted on the functional presentation of the FFT algorithms (or wavelets), on functional aspects of the automatic differentiation [2], etc. We gave projects on the simulation of waveguide models of musical sound generators using lazy streams, based on our paper [3].
- Our courses on image synthesis and processing used very intensely several functional tools for the generation of parametric surfaces and curves, and also for the texture generation, etc. Those graphical applications are the subject of this presentation.

The main idea was to abandon the forcing of the usage of functional *languages*, and to *use an existing, multi-platform, popular and free software*, possessing reasonably complete computational kernels, decent interfacing layers, and extension faculties through available libraries and user scripts (or full-fledged programs), and show how to exploit functional *style* for obtaining immediate practical results.

We decided to detach the programming style from the language, and we used the scene description languages, such as POV-Ray [4], or integrated scientific packages as Scilab as 'functionally' as possible. We exploited also Python, as a stand-alone programming tool equipped with some graphical libraries, but also as the scripting language of the 3D modelling/rendering package Blender [8]. Although Python is not an "accepted functional language", writing not too exotic programs in functional style is relatively straightforward. In this context the term 'functional' means the expression-oriented programming style, with serious usage of higher-order functionals, comprehensions (and maps) instead of loops, and — when possible — the creation of functional objects (closures) reused elsewhere. We didn't insist on the 'purity' of the basic constructions. Formerly we have tried a similar, quite satisfying, projects in an even more imperative setting – the creation and transformation of VRML scenes through scripts in Java and JavaScript. But functional techniques proved once more to be simply more elegant and more universal.

Of course, the usage of functional, as declarative as possible style was not 'implicit', but manifest. Students were reminded of techniques learnt formerly through Scheme and Haskell, even if the context contained imperative elements.

This was an experience not without danger; there were at least two lines of criticism we met:

- Typical, concrete exercices in graphics/imagery are too complicated to be solved using functional approach only without severe inefficiencies. The programming style becomes eclectic, polluted by some imperative constructs, which goes against the didactic aims of the project.

- Students see that practical functional programming is feasible using various languages, which may decrease the popularity of specifically functional languages even more...

Those issues remain open, but we noticed that the productivity of students increased substantially, when they learned how to combine functional methods with object-oriented tools. As said above, we didn't forbid such imperative forms as loops for basic constructs, but we encouraged the students to hide them in various map- or fold-like constructs.

In our opinion this liberal attitude was a good decision. It is easier to appreciate some programming paradigms, when one does not feel constrained by them. People convinced that the functional *style* is nice and powerful in practical contexts, accept easier the idea that languages which insist on this style are good ones as well...

We underline once more that we were **not** interested in teaching of FP, but on using functional tools practically. In the concerned domain we insisted on close relation between functional entities and graphical objects, on combination and transformation thereof. We avoided too complicated constructs, the abstraction level used was rather moderate.

2. Using POV-Ray as a Functional Language

2.1 Simple recursion

A standard game showing the power of recursion is the creation of fractals (von Koch or IFS style). It took the students 10 minutes to convert from Scheme the program which generates the "fern" in Fig. 1.

```
#macro Fern(p0,p1,r,n)
 #if (n=0) cone{p0,r,p1,0.8*r}
 #else
  #local n1=n-1;
  #local d=p1-p0;  #local p2=p0+0.5*d;

  union{cone{p0,r,p1,0.8*r}
   Fern(p2,p2+0.4*vrotate(d,-45*z),0.9*r,n1)
   Fern(p1,p1+0.3*vrotate(d,45*z),0.8*r,n1)
   Fern(p1,p1+0.9*vrotate(d,3*z),0.8*r,n1)}
#end  #end
```

Figure 1. A "fern" in POV-Ray

Then, it was a matter of less than one hour to model a more realistic model, such as on the Fig. 2, and created by the following recursive macro:

```
#macro Obj(a,c)
 object{Rectree(i+1,l1,s1)
        rotate Rz rotate (a+20*R)*y
        translate c*l1*y}
#end
#macro Rectree(i,l,s)
 #if(i<imax)
  #local l1=l*r;
  #local s1=s*w;
  #local R=2*rand(S)-1;
  #local Rz=(30+10*R)*z;

  union{cone{<0,0,0>,s,<0,l1,0>,s1
        texture{T_Wood7}}
    Obj(40,1) Obj(130,0.8) Obj(220,0.75)
    Obj(310,0.667)}
 #else
  triangle{<0,0,0>, <1,0,1>, <-1,1,0>
      scale 22*s1 pigment{color Green}}
 #end
#end
```

Figure 2. A recursive tree

This program served also to pinpoint the essential difference between true functions and macros: the auxiliary macro `Obj` uses *literally* identifiers which are semantically internal to `Rectree` although `Obj` is external to it. Lexical substitution is not the same as the binding of local variables. Several errors produced during the extension of this program, adding more variations, improving leaves, etc., finally gave rise to a complete project whose aim was to write in *another language* the generator of trees for POV-Ray. Most students — almost obviously — chose a functional language!

The recursive macros, with local variables make POV-Ray an ***almost*** functional language. Globally, being a scene description language, POV-Ray has naturally a declarative flavour. There are anonymous functions, and conditional expressions ("C" style: `Bool ? thnxpr : elsxpr`). The recursive instances return "values", POV-Ray objects, which may be composed, transformed, decorated (e.g., textured), etc. Of course, the "composition" of 3D objects (e.g., the Constructive Solid Geometry operations: union, difference, blending etc.) is not the same as the functional composition, they are *data* combinations, but the relation between the two is pedagogically meaningful.

POV-Ray is not a full-fledged functional language, the higher-order programming is somehow clumsy, mainly because of scoping problems. Functions are not recursive, macros are, and the lexical substitution demands much attention to avoid identifier trapping errors. But a macro can assign a parameter and thus, implicitly return a function assigned to this parameter. Many functional tools are implementable, but it is obvious that the students **must** be acquainted with the "true" functional techniques and languages first!

Here we focussed on simple recursion, and on the construction of complicated geometrical distributions, permitting the deformation of implicit surfaces, or the deformation of randomly generated configurations, like the "galaxy" in Fig. 3.

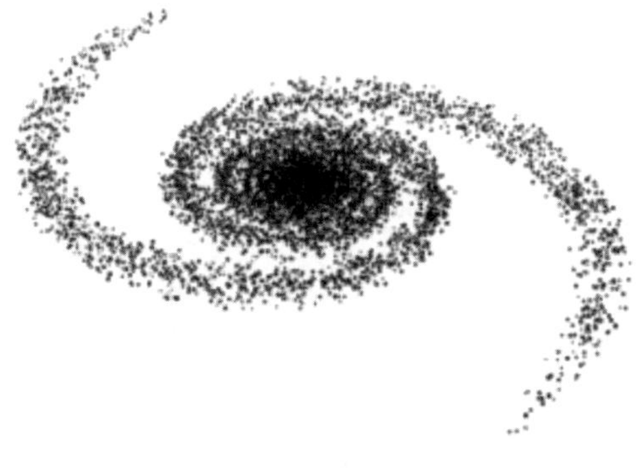

Figure 3. A "galaxy" in POV-Ray

2.2 Deformations

We did a lot more, e.g., constructing small functional L-system packages, or experimenting with various deforming/blending strategies for implicit surfaces [5] represented as equations $F(x, y, z) = 0$. (Actually, $F(x, y, z)$ represents a bit more than the surface: it splits the space into the "interior" with $F(x, y, z) < 0$, and the exterion for F positive.)

For example, in order to make an object (here: a box) distorted by an axial torsion as in Fig. 4, we programmed

```
#macro Torsion(p,fnobj) //fnobj is a funct. obj.
 #local rotx=function{x*cos(p*y)+z*sin(p*y)}
 #local rotz=function{-x*sin(p*y)+z*cos(p*y)}

 isosurface{
  function{fnobj(rotx(x,y,z),y,rotz(x,y,z))}}
#end

// (Extruded square)
#declare bbox=function{max(abs(x)-1,abs(z)-1)}

Torsion(1.4,bbox)
```

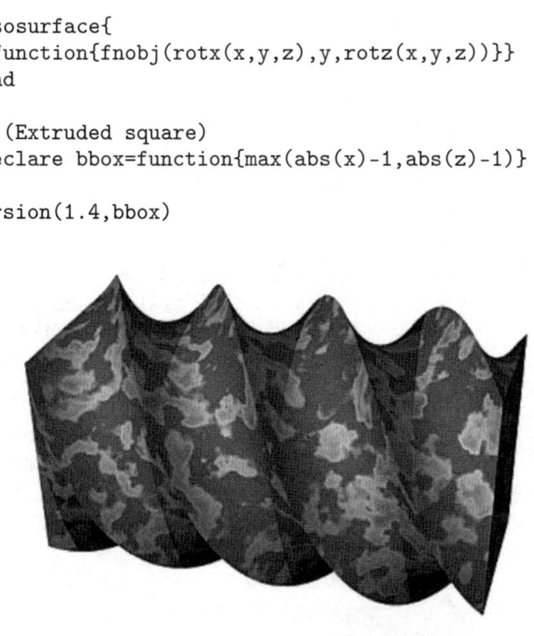

Figure 4. A screw as implicit surface

Of course, the same macro could add torsion to other implicit (iso-) surfaces. Dozen of other distortions have been proposed and implemented. It was an occasion to learn the fact that if we want that the points $\vec{x}$ composing a figure undergo a transformation $\vec{x} \longrightarrow \mathbb{R}\vec{x}$, then the surface represented as $F(\vec{x}) = 0$ must be transformed contra-variantly, and changes into $F(\mathbb{R}^{-1}\vec{x}) = 0$. This means unfortunately that several useful distortions are difficult to implement because finding the inverse transform may be very complicated, but it was an occasion to use iterative approximations.

2.3 Blending

A particularly interesting subject was the functional construction of the CSG objects: union or intersection of implicit surfaces, with blending (smoothing) functions, which produced the effects like that on Fig. 5.

Figure 5. Blended union of two cylinders

Several interesting examples have been based on the s.c. R-functions proposed by Rvachev [6]. For example, if F_1 and F_2 represent two implicit surfaces, then $F = F_1 + F_2 - \sqrt{F_1^2 + F_2^2}$ is their union. Adding to this form a term which is very small everywhere apart from the region where F_1 *and* F_2 are close to zero, e.g. $d(F_1, F_2) = a_0/(1 + (F_1/a_1)^2 + (F_2/a_2)^2)$, or some Gaussian, the transition between functions is smoothed. In order to vary a little the procedure, we coded the blended union using the Ricci approach [7]: $f = (f_1^{-k} + f_2^{-k})^{-1/k}$, where f is a function whose value at the surface is equal to 1. So, for the standard representation, the POV-Ray program which generated the Fig. 5 took the form:

```
#declare axcyl=function(a,b){a*a+b*b-1}
#declare cylx=function{axcyl(y,z)}
#declare cyly=function{axcyl(x,z)}

#macro Blend(f1,f2,k)
 #local g1=function{f1(x,y,z)+1}
 #local g2=function{f2(x,y,z)+1}

 function{
  pow(pow(g1(x,y,z),-k)+
      pow(g2(x,y,z),-k),-1/k)-1}
#end
```

```
isosurface {
  Blend(cylx,cyly,1.7)
  ...
}
```

The CSG objects exist in POV-Ray as language-embedded constructs. But we taught image synthesis *algorithms* and their implementation, not the usage of POV-Ray, so a higher level reconstruction of some techniques served the same purpose as the construction of meta-interpreters of Lisp or Prolog in those languages. (In fact, a full ray-tracer may be and has been constructed in the language of POV-Ray, but this was not so interesting from the declarative point of view).

To summarize, the language of POV-Ray permits to define generic constructions, parameterized, recursive macros, and arbitrary composition of functions which represent implicit (or parametric) surfaces. The declarative style of scene definition is natural, and inspiring. In case of more complicated programs, which become too inefficient, the *natural* solution is to construct *functional* programs in any "decent" language, whose output is a scene specification for POV-Ray. We can say thus that the second line of the criticism of our approach – that students will not use functional languages, having other tools at their disposal – is not so serious.

3. Blender and Python

3.1 Recursion and comprehensions

We got some practical experience using Python scripts for driving the 3D modelling/rendering package Blender [8]. Since Blender is an interactive modeller, we might suppose that constructing a fractal pyramid, like this in Fig. 6 is a rather painful task, while a recursive script producing it is straightforward, provided we know how to displace (and scale) 3D objects. (We must acknowledge that straightforward is not synonymous with trivial...)

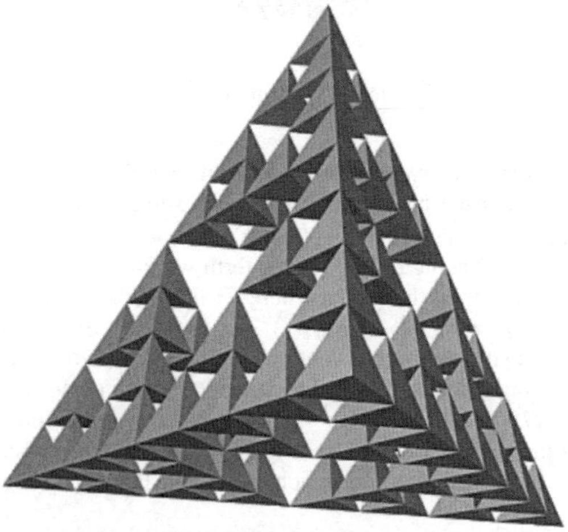

Figure 6. Sierpiński pyramid in Blender

The essential code for this object begins with an auxiliary function which 'adds' two tuples element-wise. Note the usage of pattern matching. Actually the addition in our example is the concatenation, since the elements of the tuple are two lists, containing the vertices and the facettes of tetrahedra returned by the (omitted) function `tetra`. The recursive clause is as horrible as is to be expected from a functional program which uses in one expression two maps (list comprehensions) in the form `[f(z) for z in zlist]`, and the combinator `reduce` (in Haskell: `fold`). The parameter `lp` is a list of position of vertices of a tetrahedron; they define the positions of the recursive instances of the Sierpiński sponge. We believe that it is one of the shortest programs we have seen, which generates this object...

```
def sp((a,b),(c,d)):
    return (a+c,b+d)

def sierpyr1(n,lp):
   if n==0:
      return tetra(lp)
   else:
      return
       reduce(sp,
              [sierpyr1(n-1,[p+lp[k]
                            for p in lp])
               for k in range(0,4)],
              ([],[]))
```

3.2 Closure export

However, in this context we wanted much more than just a recursion, we wanted to exploit seriously some generic, higher-order programming. The construction of parametric curves and surfaces is a particularly good target for such methods, especially if we prefer to convey algorithms *easy to memorize*, rather than "raw" and boring, although more efficient. How to construct a curve $c(t)$, a vector function of one parameter, which is a cubic spline passing between the points p_0 and p_1 for t in $(0, 1)$?

Almost all students can reconstruct in 15 minutes a *quadratic* spline passing through 3 given points, but higher polynomials are much more cumbersome. The functional solution is particularly simple and intuitive. We can construct a cubic function by the linear interpolation of two quads. Here the possibility of export a closure from a function is very useful. Here is the whole code permitting to construct `c = cubic(pm,p0,p1,p2)`. The functions `quad` and `cubic` are constructors (generators) of functional objects representing the curves, not the curves themselves. The points p_m, p_0, p_1, p_2 are knots, values of the curve for $t - 1, 0, 1, 2$.

```
def quad(pm,p0,p1):
  a,b = 0.5*(p1-pm),0.5*(p1+pm)-p0
  def q(t):
    return p0+t*(a+b*t)
  return q
def cubic(pm,p0,p1,p2):
  def c(t):
    return (1-t)*quad(pm,p0,p1)(t)+
          t*quad(p0,p1,p2)(t-1)
 return c
```

The pattern: construct (`def`) `f(x)` inside another function, and return `f` from it, became ubiquitous in Python. Not only in our exercices, but in the world of Python programmers working in scientific (and some other) domains. Despite the manifest attitude of some creators of Python, who want to remove too much of "functionalisms" for the sake of the simplification of the language, we believe that one of the reasons for its success is a reasonably good functional layer... The translation of a curve along an axis goes as follows:

```
def transl1(cv,ax,a):
    def f(t):
        return a*ax+cv(t)
    return f
```

We defined, of course, also the translation and the rotation of surfaces, and other lifted operations. Python has anonymous functions (lambdas), it can simulate conditional expressions through the Boolean shortcuts, e.g., `a = Btest and thxpr or elsxpr`, it has list functionals such as map, filter and reduce (fold), the list/generator comprehensions, and the last versions have rationalized the scope issues permitting to export closures in a straightforward, secure way. Here is another example, a spiral:

```
def spiral(r,dz):
    def f(t):
        return Vec(r*cos(t),r*sin(t),dz*t)
    return f
```

We see here that the function returns a Python *object* — a 3D vector for which we constructed a relatively complete library of basic operations, including rotations, scalar products, etc. The call to the function `cubic` returns such vector, but note that within the definition of this function this is not explicit. The dynamic, object-oriented typing of Python facilitates the coding; it suffices that such values as `p0` etc., may be added or multiplied by scalars.

3.3 Parametric surfaces

In such a way, after having constructed a library containing e.g., the rotation of a vector about an axis: `rot(v,ax,angle)`, the definition of a figure of revolution, a *parametric surface* which is a function of two parameters - coordinates:

- a parameter along the generator, the curve which will sweep the space by rotating about the axis, and
- the angle of this rotation,

becomes quite straightforward.

We define not directly the surface, but — as in the case of curves — its *constructor* (or: generator, but we don't want to confuse this term with the generating curve...), specified by this generating curve `cv` and the axis `ax`. Here is the construction of this generic revolution constructor:

```
def revol(cv,ax):
  def f(s,phi):
    return rot(cv(s),ax,phi)
  return f
```

Making a generalized cylinder, or a linear extrusion of a generator curve along an axis is even simpler. Again, a constructor:

```
def extrude(cv,ax):
  def f(s,t):
    return t*ax+cv(s)
  return f
```

Being able in such a way to 'lift' vector operations onto the domain of functions, permits to compose those operations quite easily. Here is the canonically oriented torus, with its axis along z (`AZ`).

```
def torus(rr,r):
    gen=transl1(crotate(circle(r),AX,PI/2),
                AX,rr)
    return revol(gen,AZ)
```

Such sea-shell as in Fig. 7 is a program of 5 lines, provided we use another function from our library, the Catmull-Rom spline which iterates `cubic` over a list of points specifying this splite.

```
def catrom(lp):
    pm=quad(lp[2],lp[1],lp[0])(2)
    pp=quad(lp[-3],lp[-2],lp[-1])(2)
    lp=[pm]+lp+[pp]
    fp=[cubic(lp[n],lp[n+1],lp[n+2],lp[n+3])
        for n in range(0,len(lp)-3)]
    def f(t):
        k=int(t)
        return fp[k](t-k)
    return f
```

Note the usage of list comprehension, and also of the fact that we constructed a *list of functions*. The result returned by this constructor is a closure which selects the appropriate segment function according to the parameter. This is commented below.

The transformation of the generating curve is a homothety composed with rotation. Concretely, the generating curve upon the rotation by the angle φ is scaled by the amount $\exp(\kappa\cdot\varphi)$. The origin of the coordinate system is the singular point, the top of the shell, so this scaling translates the curve.

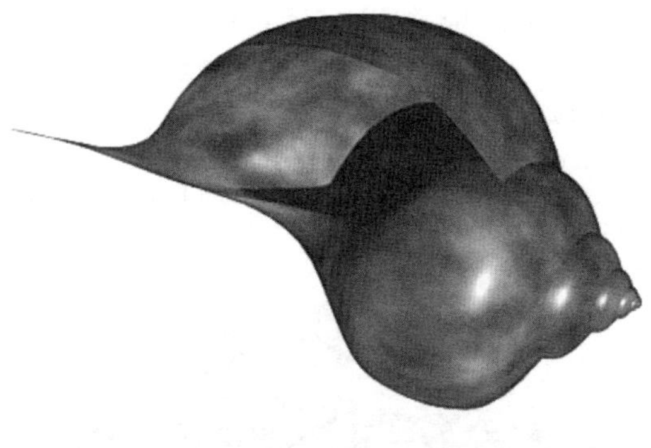

Figure 7. A sea-shell in Blender

Dozens of other sea-shells, snails, etc. have been generated. We used those functional contraptions not only to generate, but also to deform other functional surfaces, such as the deformed sphere in Fig. 8. The generic deformation functional of a surface `sf` through

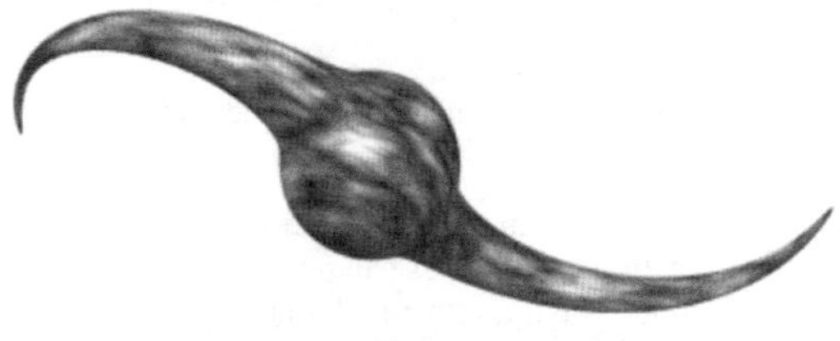

Figure 8. A deformed sphere

a function `df` which acts on points, is as simple as that:

```
def deform(sf,df):
    def f(s,t):
        p=sf(s,t)
        return df(p)
    return f
```

The deforming function was a composition of an elongation in z: $z \rightarrow z\cdot(1+fe^{-\alpha(x^2+y^2)})$, and a rotation, whose angle depended on the transversal radius: x^2+z^2; a similar function was used to create the "galaxy".

Many other generic constructs are easily programmable, for example the surfaces which interpolate between two curves:

```
def intpol(c1,c2):
    def sf(s,t):
        return (1-t)*c1(s) + t*c2(s)
    return sf
```

Other constructions, such as the Coons, 4-curves interpolation surfaces, are equally easy. Already some years ago we tried to use such techniques quite intensely [9], but we wanted then to exploit the elegance of a *typed* functional language (Clean). Since the interfacing, the 3D plotting, texturing, etc. was a bit painful, we used Clean to generate sampled points and other data stored in a file, and plotted then by Matlab (or Scilab). We observe that the current approach is easier, more comfortable for students (less tools to master). The dynamic typing offered by Python plays here a positive role, despite the known advantages of static typing for the debugging, which in a pedagogical context is a severe headache....

We acknowledge the existence of other projects combining several tools, for example the nice package Haven [10] of Anthony Courtney, which combines Haskell as a generating tool with Java for the rendering of the Scalable Vector Graphics scene descriptions.

3.4 Surfaces out of surfaces

Construction of a knot, like in Fig. 9 is not extremely easy, even if the students are told that this is a tube which follow the 'director' curve which wraps around a torus.

Figure 9. A toroidal knot in Blender

There are three ingredients in this construction, all three functional. First, we make a torus as a classical revolution surface, whose generator is a circle. Then, a *curve* is defined by constraining the torus angular parameters (ϑ, φ): $\vartheta = 2/3 \cdot \varphi$, and finally a *tube* is constructed with this curve as its director, and any generator, e.g., a square.

The construction of squares, of general splines, and other curves defined segment by segment was another exercise in functional programming. If the call to the functional generator `sg(p0,p1)` returns a curve function — the straight line passing by the specified points, the generator of the square take four corners, and constructs a *list of functions*: `sq=[sg(p0,p1, sg(p1,p2), sg(p2,p3), sg(p3,p0)]`. Then for t in $[0, 4]$ we take `k=int(t)`, and we return `sq[k](t-k)`, avoiding all case analysis. This is conceptually quite trivial, but convincing students that the construction of data containing functional objects is natural and useful, takes some time. When they grasp this idea, the functional construction of L-systems becomes considerably easier.

The example above, the construction of tubes posed another pedagogical challenge. A tubular object is a useful generic construction, which takes two curves, the generator and the director, and one fixed vector `n`, typically a normal to the generator plane. Then the generator is translated along the director, and rotated in such a way that synchronously rotated `n` coincides with the local tangent of the director. There are two distinct problems here, the construction of the tangent, and the choice of the axis/angle of rotation.

We could thus apply the strategy already known — making a functional which takes a function as parameter, and returns another function, its derivative computed numerically. The rotation problem *is* a challenge, requiring a decent knowledge of the Frenet frame computations, permitting to adopt a strategy which avoids too much torsion (which is visible in Fig. 9). We couldn't enter the full game of differential geometry, but several functional constructs which specified normals, etc. have been proposed. Although we couldn't develop the technique, we mentioned the possibility to use the *automatic differentiation technique* to compute the gradients [2]. Our surface constructor library contains this module implemented in Python as well.

We wanted to be able to use standard arithmetic operators for functions, so that `f=f1+f2` mean `f(t) = f1(t)+f2(t)`, etc. But Python does not permit such overloading of the addition operator, so we applied a known trick — Python *objects* have been constructed, for which we could define those overloaded operators (the functions `__add__` etc.), and also we overloaded the `__call__` methods permitting the object `q` to act as a function: the form `q(x)` is converted by the compiler into `q.__call__(x)`. The effective function was embedded within such an object, and invoked indirectly through the overloaded `__call__`. Then, the codes for the extrusion objects, etc. become significantly shorter.

We were thus able to convince the students on a practical set of examples that functional and object-oriented techniques may, and should go together. This version of our vector/curve/surface library is still in an experimental stage, since our department begins right now to teach Python to computer science students in a more organized way.

3.5 Python generators and laziness

Lazy lists, trees, and other co-recursive constructions are inherent to pure functional languages, and usually absent from languages with mutable data, since the delayed evaluation in such a context leads to ambiguities. Notable exceptions are lazy streams in Scheme and in Caml, but their usage is relatively rare and restricted.

The basic idea of constructing an "infinite" data structure, defined through a recursion without terminating clause, and consumed incrementally, with the *by-need* instantiation (and memoization), can be programmed in Python, thanks to the concepts of ***generators***. How can we use them for computer graphics?

A small fragment of our course on image synthesis was devoted to the sampling/polygonization of implicit surfaces. We discussed the relevant theory (variants of the marching cubes algorithm, etc., see [5]), but we found it useful to propose a simplistic polygonizer based on octrees, in order to be able to work with implicit surfaces within Blender. The idea of a lazy functional implementation of such a polygonizer can be found in [11].

Structurally an octree is a 8-fold tree, whose root corresponds to a cube, and its branches — to the 8 smaller cubes obtained by the triple binary subdivision of the root. The algorithm starts with the embedding of the implicit surface $F(\vec{x}) = 0$ in a cube, and performing a few (1 – 2) initial subdivisions. Those sub-cubes which cut the surface, i.e. whose vertices give different signs of F are subdivided further, up to the desired precision. The cubes "inside" or "outside" remain undeveloped. The points of intersection of the surface with the cubes' edges are then assembled into polygons, and Blender does the rest.

We shall not present the whole package, just the procedure-generator which constructs an infinite octree. It is parameterized by the subdivision length, and by the root cube. A cube is an object whose attribute is `vs`, the list of vertices (coordinate vectors). Its constructor, `Cub` is parameterized by its two opposite corners.

The octree itself is an object containing the root cube and br, the list of branches, which are octrees.

```
def mkoct(n,cub):
  lfd,lfu,lbd,lbu,rfd,rfu,rbd,rbu = cub.vs
  ct=0.5*(lfd+rbu)    # The center
  br=map(lambda (v1,v2): mkoct(n+1,Cub(v1,v2)),
       [(lfd,ct),(0.5*(lfd+lfu),0.5*(lfu+rbu)),
        (0.5*(lfd+lbd),0.5*(lbd+rbu)),
        (0.5*(lfd+lbu),0.5*(lbu+rbu)),
        (0.5*(lfd+rfd),0.5*(rfd+rbu)),
        (0.5*(lfd+rfu),0.5*(rfu+rbu)),
        (0.5*(lfd+rbd),0.5*(rbd+rbu)),(ct,rbu)])
  yield Oct(n,cub,br)
```

Note the endless recursion (8-fold, inside the map functional), rarely seen outside such languages as Haskell or Clean... In fact, the presence of the keyword yield makes this procedure a *generator*. Its call, e.g., oc=mkoct(0,unitCube) returns a "suspended object", instantiated through the method call oc.next(). The consumer procedure doesn't really care about that, since it obtains the access to the k-th branch of the argument by the call b=branch(oc,k), defined as follows:

```
def branch(oc,k):
    x=oc.br[k]
    if isinstance(x,GeneratorType):
        x=x.next()
        oc.br[k]=x
    return x
```

and which ensures the development by need with memoization. Of course it *can* be done differently, but the lazy approach is compact, the case analysis during the consumption process is much simpler. The consumer procedure consume(n,F,oc) is of course sensitive to the depth n. If it is greater than the limit, the cube is split into 6 simplexes (tetrahedra), and the procedure returns the list of polygons. In the recursive case the only operation which is necessary reduces to

```
...
return sum([consume(n+1,F,branch(oc,k))
            for k in range(0,8)],[])
```

(The function sum is a generic adder, which folds the overloaded (+) operator; in the current case it is the concatenation.)

The current version of the polygonizer produces the results somehow ugly, and needs further development. The advantage of having this within such modeller as Blender is the possibility to process them further interactively.

Another project which will be developed next year consists in treating the implicit surface function as a "force field", which constrains a set of initially free particles to locations near the surface [12]. The particles can then be used for the reconstruction of a mesh, and also for texturing.

4. Functional Techniques in Image Processing

The course on image synthesis was completed by a short introduction to image processing methods. Here we have worked with the image-processing package Gimp [13], which is extensible through scripts written in Scheme (SIOD). So, in principle, the functional programming could be exercized quite extensively, although its direct applications were limited, since the aim of the course was just to introduce the basic filtering, morphological operations, and some manipulations in colour spaces (which would facilitate the segmentation).

The generation and transformation of images considered as functions $f(x, y)$ whose codomain is the pixel colour, has been extensively studied, see e.g., [14, 15], and we have shown to students several dozens of images generated by programs in Clean and in Matlab. We used them as texture patterns for the 3D synthesis.

Gimp permits to draw lines, rectangles, ellipses, etc., so we could easily construct all standard Koch-style fractals, 2D L-systems, etc. (no need to show ubiquitous examples), although in this context Gimp doesn't offer anything remarkable, as compared with fuller Scheme implementations, offering a complete graphic support, such as DrScheme [16]. It is impractical to draw figures pixel by pixel, for efficiency reasons.

On the other hand, it was rather easy to construct arbitrary functions: *gradients* which generated 1-dimensional (cartesian or polar; x, y or r) slices of grey images, which were then used as *displacement maps*. The Scheme (Script-Fu) layer in Gimp provides more than 100 useful functions. For example, a linear gradient demanded just the creation of an empty gradient object, and seting its left and right colours. The linear interpolation between was automatic.

Their usage is the following. The target image is scanned point by point, and for each pixel we accede to the pixel within the source image, which has the coordinates of the target pixel *modified* by the *value* of the corresponding pixel of the displacement map. (So, the displacement map should in general be a 2-component image).

A simple *linear* (the value of the pixel is proportional to its relevant coordinate), black-white horizontal gradient interpreted as the displacement function $f(x) = ax$, could give the displacement $x \to x + ax = (1 + a)x$, a scaling transformation.

A linear gradient in x used as the y displacement, together with its transpose acting on x, permitted to construct rotations (with some rescaling): $x \to x + ay$; $y \to y - ax$ (simultaneously) of any image. By composing the linear gradient with radial weights also defined as a gradient fonction, it was easy to obtain radially weighted rotations, effects like the right image in Fig. 10.

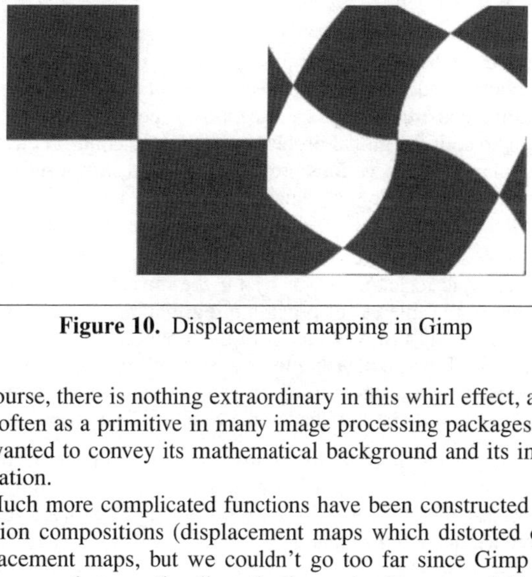

Figure 10. Displacement mapping in Gimp

Of course, there is nothing extraordinary in this whirl effect, available often as a primitive in many image processing packages. But we wanted to convey its mathematical background and its implementation.

Much more complicated functions have been constructed with function compositions (displacement maps which distorted other displacement maps, but we couldn't go too far since Gimp uses 8-bits per colour, so the discretization noise became quickly unbearable. For more consequent projects we abandoned Gimp in favour of other packages (e.g. Matlab, which unfortunately could not be distributed freely to our students). The implementation of some functional tools in Java for ImageJ [17] is under investigation. Again we shall try to convince students to *think* functionally, independently of the language used.

5. Conclusions

The usage of functional methods in computer graphics is an everlasting issue. Already in [18] we saw many interesting ideas on how to compose functional objects representing parametric graphical entities. Since then we have seen many projects in Haskell and other languages, too numerous to cite. Unfortunately, serious attempts to use functional techniques as a more or less coherent and serious teaching methodology in the domain of computer graphics seem to be rare.

Since we teach the image synthesis already for some years, the project is in constant development, but we can already say that it was an immense fun for everybody, and it occupied us for almost four months of the semester; it cannot be presented fully here. In a pedagogical context, where the time alloted to one exercise is limited, students could not concentrate themselves simultaneously on the algorithmic side of the problem, and on the interfacing. When they had to use primitive libraries (OpenGL, etc.) their visual results were too often ugly, because the programs were too simple.

By programming POV-Ray or Blender they could spend more time on the geometric design through parametrization, recursion, etc., and they could obtain something much nicer, and thus more encouraging, quite fast. We underline the fact that we had a concrete pedagogical program to realize in collaboration with other people, and we could not sacrifice the images synthesis/processing techniques just to have more time for playing with functional tools.

The curriculum of Master-1 (4-th year) in Computer Science includes a personal programming project which *should* occupy the student usually during 5 – 6 months. We delegated to those projects some more involved problems, such as the functional construction of an automatic differentiation package inspired by [2] in the context of graphics, the polygonization of implicit surfaces, and many others. Other projects, shorter but more complicated (such as the texture reconstruction using the Heeger technique [19], or the implementation of active contours — all implemented as functionally as possible) have been proposed to Master-2 (fifth year) students. This didn't work always as expected, but we can affirm the following.

- Our somewhat eclectic approach, combining the high level functional code with the necessity of implementing some imperative constructs, was a *good thing*. It permitted to our students to split the global problem in layers, to control better the interplay between various programming styles. In a sense, the functional methodology, taught formerly through Scheme and Haskell, ceased to be a "religion", and became a "weapon"...
- Because of the fact that image synthesis in general is an interesting topic to learn (it was by far the most popular optional module), the interest of programming graphic algorithms in a structured and fast way thanks to functional methods was considerable. It was a pleasure to observe that students themselves proposed such programming projects as the construction of a ray tracer, or a texturer/shader in a functional language.

So, the presented philosophy seems promising, the project will continue, and we will try to adapt it to *free* programming tools available for the students, since we do not feel restricted to any concrete language or package.

References

[1] Jerzy Karczmarczuk, *Functional Low-Level Interpreters*, Functional and Declarative Programming in Education, Pittsburgh, (2002). Available also from `www.info.unicaen.fr/~karczma/arpap/Fdpe02/fumach.pdf`.

[2] Jerzy Karczmarczuk, *Functional Differentiation of Computer Programs*, Higher-Order and Symbolic Computation **14**, pp. 35–57, (2001).

[3] Jerzy Karczmarczuk, *Functional Framework for Sound Generation*, Proceedings, Practical Aspects of Declarative Languages, PADL'05, Long Beach, Springer LNCS 3350, pp. 7–21, (2005).

[4] POV-Ray: collective work, which began with David Kirk Buck and Aaron Collins. Distribution and documentation: Web site `www.povray.org`

[5] Jules Bloomenthal (ed.), *Introduction to Implicit Surfaces*, Morgan Kauffman, (1997).

[6] V. L. Rvachev, *Theory of R-functions and Some Applications* (in Russian), Naukova Dumka, (1982). See also A. A. Pasko, V. Adzhiev, A. Sourin and V. V. Savchenko, *Function representation in geometric modeling: concepts, implementation and applications*, The Visual Computer **11**:8, pp. 429–446, (1995).

[7] A. Ricci, *A Constructive Geometry for Computer Graphics*, The Computer Journal **16**:2, pp. 157–160, (1973).

[8] Ton Roosendaal and others; Web site `http://www.blender3d.com`. See also T. Roosendaal, C. Wartmann, *The Official Blender Gamekit: Interactive 3-D for Artists*, No Starch Press, (2003).

[9] Jerzy Karczmarczuk, *Geometric Modelling in Functional Style*, Proc. of the III Latino-American Workshop on Functional Programming, CLAPF'99, Recife, Brazil, 8-9 March 1999.

[10] Antony Courtney, *HAVEN, Scalable Vector Graphics for Haskell with GCJNI and Java2D*, accessible through the Haskell Web site.

[11] Th. Zörner, P. Koopman, M. van Eekelen, R. Plasmeijer, *Polygonizing Implicit Surfaces in a Purely Functional Way*, 12 Intl. Workshop on the implementation of functional languages, IFL'00, Springer LNCS 2011, pp. 158–175, (2000).

[12] Andrew P. Witkin, PAul S. Heckbert, *Using Particles to Sample and Control Implicit Surfaces*, Procs. of the 21st SIGGRAPH Conf. on Computer Graphics and Interactive Techniques, pp. 269–277, (1994).

[13] Peter Mattis, Spencer Kimball and many others; Web site `http://www.gimp.org` for the software and the documentation (regularly updated...).

[14] Conal Elliot, *Functional Image Synthesis*, Bridges 2001 Conference: Mathematical Connections in Art, Music and Science, Winfield, July 27–29, 2001. See also *Functional Images*, a chapter in *Fun of Programming*, ed. Oege de Moor, Jeremy Gibbons, Oxford (2003).(Palgrave series Cornerstones of Computing).

[15] Jerzy Karczmarczuk *Functional Approach to Texture Generation*, PADL (2002), Portland, Springer LNCS 2257, pp. 225–242.

[16] The PLT-Scheme Web page, `www.plt-scheme.org`; full distribution and documentation.

[17] *ImageJ: Image Processing and Analysis in Java*, Web page `rsb.inf.nih.gov/ij`.

[18] Peter Henderson, *Functional Programming, Application and Implementation*, Prentice-Hall, (1980).

[19] D.J. Heeger, J.R. Bergen, *Pyramid-based Texture Analysis/Synthesis*, Procs. SIGGRAPH '95, pp. 229–239, (1995).

MinCaml: A Simple and Efficient Compiler for a Minimal Functional Language *

Eijiro Sumii
Tohoku University
sumii@ecei.tohoku.ac.jp

Abstract

We present a simple compiler, consisting of only 2000 lines of ML, for a strict, impure, monomorphic, and higher-order functional language. Although this language is minimal, our compiler generates as fast code as standard compilers like Objective Caml and GCC for several applications including ray tracing, written in the optimal style of each language implementation. Our primary purpose is education at undergraduate level to convince students—as well as average programmers—that functional languages are simple and efficient.

Categories and Subject Descriptors D.3.4 [*Programming Languages*]: Processors—Compilers; D.3.2 [*Programming Languages*]: Language Classifications—Applicative (functional) languages

General Terms Languages, Design

Keywords ML, Objective Caml, Education, Teaching

1. Introduction

The Meta Language, or ML, is a great programming language. It is one of the very few languages that achieve rather challenging and often conflicting demands—such as efficiency, simplicity, expressivity, and safety—at the same time. ML is the only language ranked within the top three *both* for efficiency (runtime speed) and for simplicity (code lines) at an informal benchmark site [2] that compares various programming language implementations. ML is also *the* language most used by the winners of the ICFP programming contests [3].

Unfortunately, however, it is also an undeniable fact that ML is a "Minor Language" in the sense that it is not as widespread as C or Perl, even though the situation is getting better thanks to mature implementations such as Objective Caml.

Why is ML not so popular? The shortest answer is: because it is not well-known! However, looking more carefully into this obvious tautology, I find that one of the reasons (among others [24]) for this "negative spiral of social inertia" is misconceptions about implementations. Nowadays, there are a number of programmers who learn ML, but they often think "I will not use it since I do not understand how it works." Or, even worse, many of them make incorrect assumptions based on arbitrary misunderstanding about implementation methods. To give a few real examples:

- "Higher-order functions can be implemented only by interpreters" (reason: they do not know function closures).
- "Garbage collection is possible only in byte code" (reason: they only know Java and its virtual machine).
- "Functional programs consume memory because they cannot reuse variables, and therefore require garbage collection" (reason: ???).

Obviously, these statements must be corrected, in particular when they are uttered from the mouths of our students.

But how? It does not suffice to give short lessons like "higher-order functions are implemented by closures," because they often lead to another myth such as "ML functions are inefficient because they are implemented by closures." (In fact, thanks to known function call optimization, ML functions are just as efficient as C functions if they can be written in C at all—except that function *pointers* can sometimes be used in more efficient ways than function closures.) In order to get rid of the essential prejudice that leads to such ill-informed utterances as above, we end up in giving a full course on how to implement an efficient compiler of a functional language. (Throughout this paper, an efficient compiler means a compiler that generates fast code, not a compiler which itself is fast.) To this goal, we need a simple but efficient compiler which can be understood even by undergraduate students or average programmers.

The MinCaml Compiler was developed for this purpose. It is a compiler from a strict, impure, monomorphic, and higher-order functional language—which itself is also called MinCaml and whose syntax is a subset of Objective Caml—to SPARC Assembly. Although it is implemented in only 2000 lines of Objective Caml, its efficiency is comparable to that of OCamlOpt (the optimizing compiler of Objective Caml) or GCC for several applications written in the optimal style of each language implementation.

Curricular Background. MinCaml has been used since year 2001 in a third-year undergraduate course at the Department of Information Science in the University of Tokyo. The course is just called Compiler Experiments (in general, we do not call courses by numbers in Japan), where students are required to implement their own compiler of the MinCaml language from scratch[1], given both high-level and medium-level descriptions in a natural language and mathematical pseudo-code (as in Section 4.3 and 4.4). Although the course schedule varies every year, a typical pattern looks like Table 1.

* The present work was supported by the Information-Technology Promotion Agency, Japan as an Exploratory Software Project.

[1] The source code of MinCaml was not publicly available until March 2005.

Week	Topics
1	Introduction, lexical analysis, parsing
2	K-normalization
3	α-conversion, β-reduction, reduction of nested `let`-expressions
4	Inline expansion, constant folding, elimination of unnecessary definitions
5	Closure conversion, known function call optimization
6	Virtual machine code generation
7	Function calling conventions
8	Register allocation
9	Register spilling
10	Assembly generation
11	Tail call optimization, continuation passing style
12	Type inference, floating-point number operations
13	Garbage collection [no implementation required]
14	Type-based analyses (case study: escape analysis) [no implementation required]

Table 1. Course Schedule

Compiler Experiments is associated with another course named Processor Experiments, where groups of students design and implement their own CPUs by using programmable LSI called FPGA (field programmable gate arrays). Then, they develop compilers for those CPUs, execute ray tracing, and compete on the speed of execution.[2] The goal of these courses is to understand how computer hardware and software work without treating them as black boxes (which leads to misconceptions).

Since students in Tokyo learn only liberal arts for the first year and half, these courses are in fact scheduled in the third *semester* of the information science major curriculum. By then, the students have learned Scheme, ML, and Prolog in addition to C/C++ and SPARC Assembly (during courses on operating systems and computer architecture) as well as Java (in the liberal arts courses). In particular, they have already learned how to write a simple interpreter for a small subset of ML.

Furthermore, they have already taken lectures on compilers of imperative languages (including standard algorithms for lexical analysis, parsing, and register allocation) for one semester. The purpose of our course is to teach efficient compilation of functional languages, rather than giving a *general* compiler course *using* functional languages.

Design Policy. Given these situations, MinCaml was designed with three requirements in mind: (1) It must be understood in every detail by undergraduate students (through 14 hours of lectures and 42 hours of programming). (2) It must be able to execute at least one non-trivial application: ray tracing. (3) It must be as efficient as standard compilers for this application and other typical small programs. Thus, it makes no sense to try to implement the full functionality of ML. To achieve our first goal, MinCaml only supports a *minimal* subset of ML sufficient to meet the other goals. In particular, we have dropped polymorphism and data types as well as modules and garbage collection, though basic implementation techniques for these features are still covered in class.

To make the compiler easier to understand, every design decision is clearly motivated, as described in the following sections.

Paper Overview. Section 2 presents the source language, MinCaml, and Section 3 discusses the design of our compiler. Section 4 elaborates on its details. Section 5 gives the results of our experiments to show the efficiency of the compiler. Section 6 compares our approach with related work and Section 7 concludes with future directions.

The implementation and documentations of MinCaml are publicly available at `http://min-caml.sf.net/index-e.html`. Readers are invited (though not required) to consult them when the present paper refers to implementation details.

[2] This competition started in 1995 and its official record was held by the author's group since they took the course in 1998 until the FPGA was upgraded in 2003.

M, N, e ::=	expressions
c	constants
$op(M_1, \ldots, M_n)$	arithmetic operations
`if` M `then` N_1 `else` N_2	conditional branches
`let` $x = M$ `in` N	variable definitions
x	variables
`let rec` $x\ y_1\ \ldots\ y_n = M$ `and` ... `in` N	function definitions
$M\ N_1\ \ldots\ N_n$	function applications
$(M_1, \ldots, M_n)$	tuple creations
`let` $(x_1, \ldots, x_n) = M$ `in` N	reading from tuples
`Array.create` $M\ N$	array creations
M_1`.`(M_2)	reading from arrays
M_1`.`$(M_2) \leftarrow M_3$	writing to arrays
ρ, σ, τ ::=	types
π	primitive types
$\tau_1 \to \ldots \to \tau_n \to \tau$	function types
$\tau_1 \times \ldots \times \tau_n$	tuple types
τ `array`	array types
α	type variables

Figure 1. Syntax of MinCaml

2. The Language

The source language of MinCaml is a minimal subset of Objective Caml, whose abstract syntax and types are given in Figure 1. This abstract syntax is designed for the following reasons. First of all, as any practical functional language does, we have basic values such as integers, floating-point numbers, booleans, tuples, and functions. Each of them requires at least one constructor (such as constants, function definitions, and tuple creations) and one destructor (such as arithmetic operations, conditional branches, function applications, and reading from tuples).

Conditional branches must be a special form since we do not have more general data types and pattern matching. Tuples are destructed using a simple form of pattern matching, instead of projections like $\#_i(M)$. This avoids the flex record problem: functions such as $f(x) = \#_1(x)$ do not have principal types in the standard type system of ML without record polymorphism [19, 22].

Higher-order functions are supported since functions can be referred to just as variables, and since nested function definitions with free variables are allowed. For simplicity, however, partial function applications are not automatically recognized by the compiler and must be explicitly written by hand, for example like `let rec` $f_3\ y = f\ 3\ y$ `in` f_3 instead of just $f\ 3$ if f is defined to take two arguments. In this respect, our language is more similar to Scheme than to ML.

Since our primary application is ray tracing, we also need arrays for efficient representation of vectors and matrices. Array construction must be a special syntactic form because it is parametric in the element type. (Objective Caml can express this by using a polymorphic library function, but MinCaml cannot.) Once we have arrays, reference cells can also be implemented as arrays with just one element. This implementation does not affect efficiency as we anyway have no boundary checks for array accesses.

The types are standard monomorphic types except for n-ary function types, which reflect the lack of partial function applications as mentioned above, and type variables, which will be used for type inference.

These abstract syntax and types are literally implemented as ML data types `Syntax.t` and `Type.t`, except that bound variables in `Syntax.t` are annotated with elements of `Type.t` to keep the type information for later use. Also, for readability, a function definition is represented by a record with three fields `name`, `args` and `body` instead of their triple.

Why Objective Caml? We have chosen Objective Caml as the meta language of MinCaml, as well as using its subset as the object language. This is just because Objective Caml is the only statically typed functional language that is taught well in our curriculum (and because static typing—in particular, exhaustiveness check of pattern matching—helps much when students write a compiler). Otherwise, either Standard ML or even Haskell would be fine as well (though laziness might affect efficiency and require more optimizations such as strictness analysis and linearity analysis).

Why no data types and no pattern matching? As already stated above, we have omitted data types (including lists) and pattern matching. This may sound disappointing, as almost all real programs in ML use them. However, we find that pattern matching is by far more complex than other features when compiling core ML. In addition, it is still possible to write interesting programs without using any data types (or patter matching), as shown in Section 5. Besides, the students are already busy enough in implementing other, more basic features such as higher-order functions. A possible alternative would be to supply a pattern matcher implemented by the instructor, but we rejected this approach because the whole point of our course was to avoid such a "black box" in the compiler.

Why no polymorphism? We have omitted polymorphism as well. Since we do not have data types at all (let alone polymorphic data types), there is much less use for polymorphic functions. In addition, polymorphic functions may affect even the efficiency of monomorphic functions (if implemented by boxing floating-point numbers, for example). On the other hand, it would not be too hard to implement polymorphic functions by code duplication (as in MLton [4]) without sacrificing efficiency. Polymorphic type inference would not be a big problem, either, because it is only a little more complex than the monomorphic version.

In the actual course, we offer brief explanation of the two basic methods above (boxing and code duplication) of implementing polymorphism. Type inference with `let`-polymorphism is taught (and implemented in a simple interpreter) in a previous course on ML programming.

Why no garbage collection? Once we have decided to drop data types, many of the interesting programs can be written in natural ways without allocating too many heap objects. As a result, they can run with no garbage collection at all.

Of course, however, garbage collection is a fundamental feature of most modern programming languages. Thus, we offer a lecture on garbage collection for 4 hours (with no programming tasks), covering basic algorithms such as reference counting, copying GC, and mark-and-sweep GC as well as more advanced topics (without too much detail) including incremental GC, generational GC, and conservative GC.

Why no array boundary checks? While it is easy to implement array boundary checks in MinCaml, we omitted them by default for fairer comparison with C (and OCamlOpt `-unsafe`) as in Section 5. Optimizing away redundant checks would be much harder, as it requires the compiler to solve integer constraints in general.

Module	LoC
Lexical analysis (in OCamlLex)	102
Parsing (in OCamlYacc)	175
Type inference	174
K-normalization	195
α-conversion	52
β-reduction	43
Reduction of nested `let`-expressions	22
Inline expansion	47
Constant folding	50
Elimination of unnecessary definitions	39
Closure conversion	136
Virtual machine code generation	208
13-Bit immediate optimization	42
Register allocation	262
Assembly generation	256

Table 2. Main Modules of The MinCaml Compiler

External functions and arrays. Unlike in ordinary ML, free variables in MinCaml programs are automatically treated as external—either external functions or external arrays—so their declarations can be omitted. This is just for simplicity: since MinCaml is simply typed, their types can easily be inferred from the programs [15].

3. The Compiler

The main modules of The MinCaml Compiler are listed in Table 2, along with their lines of code. This section discusses major choices that we have made in their design and implementation. Further details about the internal structure of MinCaml are described in Section 4.

Lexical analysis and parsing. Although syntax used to be a central issue in conventional compiler courses, we spend as little time as possible on it in our course: that is, we just give students our lexer and parser written in OCamlLex and OCamlYacc. The reason is that lexical analysis and parsing have already been taught in another compiler course (for imperative languages) in our curriculum. Possible alternatives to Lex and Yacc would be parser combinators or packrat parsing [12], but we did not adopt them as syntax is anyway out of scope.

K-normalization. After parsing (and type inference), we use K-normal forms [7] as the central intermediate language in MinCaml. K-normal forms are useful as it makes intermediate computations and their results explicit, simplifying many optimizations including inline expansion and constant folding.

We did not choose A-normal forms [11] because we did not need them: that is, A-normalizing *all* K-normal forms would help little in our compiler. On the contrary, *requiring* the intermediate code to be A-normal forms (i.e., forbidding nested `let`-expressions) complicates inline expansion.

In addition, A-normalization in the strict sense [11] eliminates all conditional branches in non-tail positions by duplicating their evaluation contexts, which can cause code explosion if applied literally. But if we allow conditional branches in non-tail positions, we lose the merit of A-normal forms that e_1 in `let` $x = e_1$ `in` e_2 is always an atomic expression (because e_1 may be a conditional branch `if` e_{11} `then` e_{12} `else` e_{13}, where e_{12} and e_{13} can themselves be `let`-expressions).

We did not choose CPS [5], either, for a similar reason: it does not allow conditional branches in non-tail positions and requires extra creation of the continuation closure (or inline expansion of it).

Inline expansion. Our algorithm for inlining is rather simple: it expands all calls to functions whose size (number of syntactic nodes in K-normal form) is less than a constant threshold given by the user. Since this does not always terminate when repeated (e.g., consider `let rec` $f\ x = f\ x$ `in` f 3), the number of iterations is also bounded by a user-given constant. Although this may seem *too* simple, it just works well for our programs—including recursive functions as well as loops implemented by tail recursion (achieving the effect of loop unrolling)—with reasonable increase of code size. By contrast, other inlining algorithms (see [20] for example) are much more complex than ours. Note that our inlining algorithm is implemented in only 47 lines, including the "size" function.

Closure conversion. MinCaml supports higher-order functions by closure conversion. It optimizes calls to known functions with no free variables. Again, this known function optimization is simple and effective enough for our purpose. Indeed, it optimizes *all* function calls in the critical parts of our benchmark applications.

In addition to K-normal form expressions, we introduce three special constructs `make_closure`, `apply_closure`, and `apply_direct` (which means known function calls) in the intermediate language after closure conversion. This enables us to keep the simple types without more advanced mechanisms such as existential types [17].

Register Allocation. The most sophisticated process in MinCaml (or perhaps in any modern compiler) is register allocation. Although many standard algorithms exist for imperative languages (e.g., [8, 21]), we find them unnecessarily complicated for MinCaml because its variables are never destructively updated, obviating the standard notion of "def-use chains" [18]. In addition, it is always better to spill a variable *as early as possible*, if at all. Thus, we have adopted a simpler greedy algorithm with backtracking (for early spilling) and look-ahead (for register targeting [5]). We need not worry about coverage, because standard algorithms have already been taught in the other compiler course (for imperative languages).

4. Inside The MinCaml Compiler

The architecture of MinCaml adheres to the following principle. A compiler, by definition, is a program that transforms high-level programs to lower-level code. For example, the ML function

```
let rec gcd m n =
  if m = 0 then n else
  if m <= n then gcd m (n - m) else
  gcd n (m - n)
```

is compiled into the SPARC Assembly code

```
gcd.7:         cmp     %i2, 0
               bne     be_else.18
               nop
               mov     %i3, %i2
               retl
               nop
be_else.18:    cmp     %i2, %i3
               bg      ble_else.19
               nop
               sub     %i3, %i2, %i3
               b       gcd.7
               nop
ble_else.19:   sub     %i2, %i3, %o5
               mov     %i3, %i2
               mov     %o5, %i3
               b       gcd.7
               nop
```

which, at a first glance, looks totally different. The MinCaml Compiler, like many other modern compiles, bridges this huge gap by defining appropriate intermediate languages and applying simple program transformations one by one. The major five gaps between MinCaml and SPARC Assembly are:

1. Types. MinCaml has a type discipline; assembly does not.
2. Nested expressions. MinCaml code is tree-structured with compound instructions; assembly code is a linear sequence of atomic instructions.
3. Nested function definitions. In MinCaml, we can define a function inside another function like
   ```
   let rec make_adder x =
     let rec adder y = x + y in
     adder in
   (make_adder 3) 7
   ```
   but assembly has only top-level "labels."
4. MinCaml has data structures such as tuples and arrays, while assembly does not.
5. In MinCaml, we can use as many variables as we want, but only a limited number of registers are available in assembly (and therefore they sometimes must be spilled to memory).

To bridge these gaps, MinCaml applies translations such as type inference, K-normalization, closure conversion, virtual machine code generation, register allocation (in this order). In what follows, we will explain the compilation processes of MinCaml including these translations and other optimizations.

4.1 Lexical Analysis and Parsing (102 + 175 Lines)

```
type Id.t (* variable names *)
type 'a M.t (* finite maps from Id.t to 'a *)
type S.t (* finite sets of Id.t *)

type Type.t (* types *)
type Syntax.t (* expressions *)
```

The lexical analysis and parsing of MinCaml are implemented with standard tools, OCamlLex and OCamlYacc. As usual, they translate a string of characters to a sequence of tokens and then to an abstract syntax tree, which is necessary for any complex program manipulation. There is nothing special to be noted: indeed, in our course, the files `lexer.mll` and `parser.mly` are just given to students in order to avoid the overhead of learning the tools themselves. The only non-trivial point—if any—is function arguments: to parse `x-3` as integer subtraction rather than function application `x(-3)`, the parser distinguishes "simple expressions" (expressions that can be function arguments with no extra parentheses) from other expressions like `-3`, just as Objective Caml does.

4.2 Type Inference (174 Lines)

```
val Typing.f : Syntax.t -> Syntax.t
val Typing.extenv : Type.t M.t ref

(* "private" function to
   destructively substitute type variables *)
val Typing.g : Type.t M.t -> Syntax.t -> Type.t
```

Since MinCaml is an implicitly typed language but our compiler relies on the code being annotated with types, we first carry out a monomorphic version of Hindley-Milner type inference. It is also implemented in a standard way, representing type variables as `Type.t option ref` and substituting `None` with `Some` τ during unification. The only deviation is our treatment of external variables: when the type checker sees a free variable not found in the type environment, this variable is assumed as "external" and added to a special type environment `Typing.extenv` for external variables. Thus, they need not be declared in advance: their types are inferred just as ordinary variables. This principal typing functionality is peculiar to MinCaml and not applicable to full ML with `let`-polymorphism [15]. After the type inference, instantiated type variables (references to `Some` τ) are replaced with their contents (type τ). Any uninstantiated type variables is defaulted (arbitrarily) to `int`.

4.3 K-Normalization (195 Lines)

```
type KNormal.t (* K-normalized expressions *)

val KNormal.f : Syntax.t -> KNormal.t
val KNormal.fv : KNormal.t -> S.t
```

We stated that compilation is about bridging the gaps between high-level programs and low-level code. One of the gaps is nested expressions: usually, a sequence of several instructions (like `add`, `add`, `add`, and `sub`) are needed to computer the value of a compound expression (like `a+b+c-d`).

This gap is bridged by a translation called *K-normalization*, which defines every intermediate result of computation as a variable. For example, the previous expression can be translated to:

```
let tmp1 = a + b in
let tmp2 = tmp1 + c in
tmp2 - d
```

In general, the process of K-normalization can be described as follows. First, we define the abstract syntax of the intermediate language, K-normal forms, which is implemented as ML data type `KNormal.t`.

$$
\begin{array}{lcl}
M, N, e & ::= & c \\
 & | & op(x_1, \ldots, x_n) \\
 & | & \texttt{if } x = y \texttt{ then } M \texttt{ else } N \\
 & | & \texttt{if } x \leq y \texttt{ then } M \texttt{ else } N \\
 & | & \texttt{let } x = M \texttt{ in } N \\
 & | & x \\
 & | & \texttt{let rec } x\ y_1\ \ldots\ y_n = M \texttt{ and } \ldots \texttt{ in } N \\
 & | & x\ y_1\ \ldots\ y_n \\
 & & \vdots
\end{array}
$$

The main point is that every target of basic operations—such as arithmetic operations, function applications, tuple creations, and reading from tuples—is now a variable, not a nested expression, because nested expressions are converted into sequences of `let`-expressions as in the example above. This conversion can be described by the following function $\mathcal{K}$. For every equation in this definition, all variables not appearing on the left-hand side are freshly generated. Although this function is straightforward, it is presented here for the purpose of showing how the mathematical pseudo-code given to students (and required to be implemented in Objective Caml, as mentioned in Section 1) looks like in general.

$$
\begin{array}{l}
\mathcal{K}(c) = c \\
\mathcal{K}(op(M_1, \ldots, M_n)) = \\
\quad \texttt{let } x_1 = \mathcal{K}(M_1) \texttt{ in} \\
\quad \ldots \\
\quad \texttt{let } x_n = \mathcal{K}(M_n) \texttt{ in} \\
\quad op(x_1, \ldots, x_n) \\
\mathcal{K}(\texttt{if } M_1 = M_2 \texttt{ then } N_1 \texttt{ else } N_2) = \\
\quad \texttt{let } x = \mathcal{K}(M_1) \texttt{ in let } y = \mathcal{K}(M_2) \texttt{ in} \\
\quad \texttt{if } x = y \texttt{ then } \mathcal{K}(N_1) \texttt{ else } \mathcal{K}(N_2) \\
\mathcal{K}(\texttt{if } M_1 \neq M_2 \texttt{ then } N_1 \texttt{ else } N_2) = \\
\quad \mathcal{K}(\texttt{if } M_1 = M_2 \texttt{ then } N_2 \texttt{ else } N_1) \\
\mathcal{K}(\texttt{if } M_1 \leq M_2 \texttt{ then } N_1 \texttt{ else } N_2) = \\
\quad \texttt{let } x = \mathcal{K}(M_1) \texttt{ in let } y = \mathcal{K}(M_2) \texttt{ in} \\
\quad \texttt{if } x \leq y \texttt{ then } \mathcal{K}(N_1) \texttt{ else } \mathcal{K}(N_2) \\
\mathcal{K}(\texttt{if } M_1 \geq M_2 \texttt{ then } N_1 \texttt{ else } N_2 = \\
\quad \mathcal{K}(\texttt{if } M_2 \leq M_1 \texttt{ then } N_1 \texttt{ else } N_2) \\
\mathcal{K}(\texttt{if } M_1 > M_2 \texttt{ then } N_1 \texttt{ else } N_2) = \\
\quad \mathcal{K}(\texttt{if } M_1 \leq M_2 \texttt{ then } N_2 \texttt{ else } N_1) \\
\mathcal{K}(\texttt{if } M_1 < M_2 \texttt{ then } N_1 \texttt{ else } N_2) = \\
\quad \mathcal{K}(\texttt{if } M_2 \leq M_1 \texttt{ then } N_2 \texttt{ else } N_1) \\
\mathcal{K}(\texttt{if } M \texttt{ then } N_1 \texttt{ else } N_2) = \\
\quad \mathcal{K}(\texttt{if } M = \texttt{false then } N_2 \texttt{ else } N_1) \\
\qquad \text{(if } M \text{ is not a comparison)} \\
\mathcal{K}(\texttt{let } x = M \texttt{ in } N) = \\
\quad \texttt{let } x = \mathcal{K}(M) \texttt{ in } \mathcal{K}(N) \\
\mathcal{K}(x) = x \\
\mathcal{K}(\texttt{let rec } f\ x_1\ \ldots\ x_n = M \texttt{ and } \ldots \texttt{ in } N) = \\
\quad \texttt{let rec } f\ x_1\ \ldots\ x_n = \mathcal{K}(M) \texttt{ and } \ldots \texttt{ in } \mathcal{K}(N) \\
\mathcal{K}(M\ N_1\ \ldots\ N_n) = \\
\quad \texttt{let } x = \mathcal{K}(M) \texttt{ in} \\
\quad \texttt{let } y_1 = \mathcal{K}(N_1) \texttt{ in} \\
\quad \ldots \\
\quad \texttt{let } y_n = \mathcal{K}(N_n) \texttt{ in} \\
\quad x\ y_1\ \ldots\ y_n \\
\quad \vdots
\end{array}
$$

As apparent from the definitions above, we also translate conditional branches into two special forms combining comparisons and branches. This translation bridges another gap between MinCaml and assembly where branch instructions must follow compare instructions. Although unrelated to K-normalization, it is implemented here to avoid introducing yet another intermediate language.

In addition, as an optional optimization, our actual implementation avoids inserting a `let`-expression if the term is already a variable. This small improvement is implemented in auxiliary function `insert_let`.

```
let insert_let (e, t) k =
  match e with
  | Var(x) -> k x
  | _ ->
      let x = Id.gentmp t in
      let e', t' = k x in
      Let((x, t), e, e'), t'
```

It takes an expression `e` (with its type `t`) and a continuation `k`, generates a variable `x` if `e` is not already a variable, applies `k` to `x` to obtain the body `e'` (with its type `t'`), inserts a `let`-expression to bind `x` to `e`, and returns it (with `t'`). The types are passed around just because they are necessary for type annotations of bound variables, and are not essential to K-normalization itself.

This trick not only improves the result of K-normalization but also simplifies its implementation. (This would be yet another evidence that continuations are relevant to `let`-insertion [16] in general.) For example, the case for integer addition can be coded as

```
(* in pattern matching over Syntax.t *)
| Syntax.Add(e1, e2) ->
    insert_let (g env e1)
```

```
        (fun x -> insert_let (g env e2)
            (fun y -> Add(x, y), Type.Int))
```

and reading from arrays as:

```
| Syntax.Get(e1, e2) ->
    (match g env e1 with
    | (_, Type.Array(t)) as g_e1 ->
        insert_let g_e1
          (fun x -> insert_let (g env e2)
              (fun y -> Get(x, y), t))
    | _ -> assert false)
```

The false assertion in the last line could be removed if K-normalization were fused with type inference, but we rejected this alternative in favor of modularity.

4.4 α-Conversion (52 Lines)

```
val Alpha.f : KNormal.t -> KNormal.t

(* also public for reuse by Inline.g *)
val Alpha.g : Id.t M.t -> KNormal.t -> KNormal.t
```

Following K-normalization, MinCaml renames all bound variables of a program to fresh names, which is necessary for the correctness of transformations such as inlining. It can be specified by the following function α, where variables not appearing on the left-hand side are freshly generated and $\varepsilon(x)$ is defined to be x when x is not in the domain of ε.

$$
\begin{array}{l}
\alpha_\varepsilon(c) = c \\
\alpha_\varepsilon(op(x_1,\ldots,x_n)) = \\
\quad op(\varepsilon(x_1),\ldots,\varepsilon(x_n)) \\
\alpha_\varepsilon(\texttt{if } x = y \texttt{ then } M_1 \texttt{ else } M_2) = \\
\quad \texttt{if } \varepsilon(x) = \varepsilon(y) \texttt{ then } \alpha_\varepsilon(M_1) \texttt{ else } \alpha_\varepsilon(M_2) \\
\alpha_\varepsilon(\texttt{if } x \le y \texttt{ then } M_1 \texttt{ else } M_2) = \\
\quad \texttt{if } \varepsilon(x) \le \varepsilon(y) \texttt{ then } \alpha_\varepsilon(M_1) \texttt{ else } \alpha_\varepsilon(M_2) \\
\alpha_\varepsilon(\texttt{let } x = M \texttt{ in } N) = \\
\quad \texttt{let } x' = \alpha_\varepsilon(M) \texttt{ in } \alpha_{\varepsilon, x\mapsto x'}(N) \\
\alpha_\varepsilon(x) = \varepsilon(x) \\
\alpha_\varepsilon(\texttt{let rec } f\ x_1\ \ldots\ x_m = M_1 \\
\quad \texttt{and } g\ y_1\ \ldots\ y_n = M_2 \\
\quad \ldots \\
\quad \texttt{in } N) = \\
\quad \texttt{let rec } f'\ x'_1\ \ldots\ x'_m = \alpha_{\varepsilon,\sigma,x_1\mapsto x'_1,\ldots,x_m\mapsto x'_m}(M_1) \\
\quad \texttt{and } g'\ y'_1\ \ldots\ y'_n = \alpha_{\varepsilon,\sigma,y_1\mapsto y'_1,\ldots,y_n\mapsto y'_n}(M_2) \\
\quad \ldots \\
\quad \texttt{in } \alpha_{\varepsilon,\sigma}(N) \qquad (\text{where } \sigma = f \mapsto f', g \mapsto g', \ldots) \\
\alpha_\varepsilon(x\ y_1\ \ldots\ y_n) = \\
\quad \varepsilon(x)\ \varepsilon(y_1)\ \ldots\ \varepsilon(y_n) \\
\vdots
\end{array}
$$

It is implemented by a recursive function `Alpha.g`, which takes a (sub-)expression with a mapping ε from old names to new names and returns an α-converted expression. If a variable is not found in the mapping, it is considered external and left unchanged. This behavior is implemented by auxiliary function `Alpha.find`, which is used everywhere in `Alpha.g` since variables are ubiquitous in K-normal forms.

Naturally, as long as we are just α-converting a whole program, we only need to export the interface function `Alpha.f` which calls `Alpha.g` with an empty mapping. Nevertheless, the internal function `Alpha.g` is also exported because it is useful for inlining as explained later.

4.5 β-Reduction (43 Lines)

```
val Beta.f : KNormal.t -> KNormal.t

(* private *)
val Beta.g : Id.t M.t -> KNormal.t -> KNormal.t
```

It is often useful—both for clarify and for efficiency—to reduce expressions such as `let` $x = y$ `in` $x + y$ to $y + y$, expanding the aliasing of variables. We call the expansion *β-reduction* of K-normal forms. (Of course, this name originates from β-reduction in λ-calculus, of which ours is a special case if `let`-expressions are represented by applications of λ-abstractions, like $(\lambda x.\, x + y)y$ for example.) It is not always necessary in ordinary programs, but is sometimes effective after other transformations.

β-reduction in MinCaml is implemented by function `Beta.g`, which takes an expression with a mapping from variables to equal variables and returns the β-reduced expression. Specifically, when we see an expression of the form `let` $x = e_1$ `in` e_2, we first β-reduce e_1. If the result is a variable y, we add the mapping from x to y and then continue by β-reducing e_2. Again, since variables appear everywhere in K-normal forms, auxiliary function `Beta.find` is defined and used for brevity (as in α-conversion) to substitute variables if and only if they are found in the mapping.

4.6 Reduction of Nested `let`-Expressions (22 Lines)

```
val Assoc.f : KNormal.t -> KNormal.t
```

Next, in order to expose the values of nested `let`-expressions for subsequent transformations, we flatten nested `let`-expressions such as `let` $x =$ (`let` $y = e_1$ `in` e_2) `in` $e3$ to `let` $y = e_1$ `in let` $x = e_2$ `in` $e3$. This "reduction" by itself does not affect the efficiency of programs compiled by MinCaml, but it helps other optimizations (e.g., constant folding of e_2) as well as simplifying the intermediate code.

This transformation is implemented by function `Assoc.f`. Upon seeing an expression of the form `let` $x = e_1$ `in` e_2, we first reduce e_1 to e'_1 and e_2 to e'_2 by recursion. Then, if e'_1 is of the form `let ... in` e, we return the expression `let ... in let` $x = e$ `in` e'_2. This verbal explanation may sound tricky but the actual implementation is simple:

```
(* in pattern matching over KNormal.t *)
| Let(xt, e1, e2) ->
    let rec insert = function
      | Let(yt, e3, e4) ->
          Let(yt, e3, insert e4)
      | LetRec(fundefs, e) ->
          LetRec(fundefs, insert e)
      | LetTuple(yts, z, e) ->
          LetTuple(yts, z, insert e)
      | e -> Let(xt, e, f e2) in
    insert (f e1)
```

Indeed, `assoc.ml` consists of only 22 lines as noted above.

4.7 Inline Expansion (47 Lines)

```
val Inline.threshold : int ref
val Inline.f : KNormal.t -> KNormal.t

(* private *)
val Inline.size : KNormal.t -> int
val Inline.g : ((Id.t * Type.t) list * KNormal.t) M.t ->
               KNormal.t -> KNormal.t
```

The next optimization is the most effective one: inline expansion. It replaces calls to small functions with their bodies. MinCaml implements it in module `Inline` as follows.

Upon seeing a function definition `let rec` $f\ x_1\ \ldots\ x_n = e$ `in ...`, we compute the size of e by `Inline.size`. If this size is less than the value of integer reference `Inline.threshold` set by the user, we add the mapping from function name f to the pair of formal arguments $x_1, \ldots, x_n$ and body e. Then, upon seeing a function call $f\ y_1\ \ldots\ y_n$, we look up the formal arguments $x_1, \ldots, x_n$ of f and its body e, and return e with $x_1, \ldots, x_n$ substituted by $y_1, \ldots, y_n$.

However, since inlined expressions are copies of function bodies, their variables may be duplicated and therefore must be α-converted again. Fortunately, the previous process of substituting formal arguments with actual arguments can be carried out by Alpha.g together with α-conversion, just by using the correspondence from $x_1, \ldots, x_n$ to $y_1, \ldots, y_n$ (instead of an empty mapping) as the initial mapping. Thus, the inline expansion can be implemented just as

```
(* pattern matching over KNormal.t *)
| App(x, ys) when M.mem x env ->
    let (zs, e) = M.find x env in
    let env' =
      List.fold_left2
        (fun env' (z, t) y -> M.add z y env')
        M.empty zs ys in
    Alpha.g env' e
```

where M is a module for mappings.

4.8 Constant Folding (50 Lines)

```
val ConstFold.f : KNormal.t -> KNormal.t

(* private *)
val ConstFold.g : KNormal.t M.t -> KNormal.t -> KNormal.t
```

Once functions are inlined, many operations have arguments whose values are already known, as $x+y$ in let $x = 3$ in let $y = 7$ in $x+y$. Constant folding carries out such operations at compile-time and replaces them with constants like 10. MinCaml implements it in function ConstFold.g. It takes an expression with a mapping from variables to their definitions, and returns the expression after constant folding. For example, given an integer addition $x + y$, it examines whether the definitions of x and y are integer constants. If so, it calculates the result and returns it right away. Conversely, given a variable definition let $x = e$ in ..., it adds the mapping from x to e. This is applied to floating-point numbers and tuples as well.

4.9 Elimination of Unnecessary Definitions (39 Lines)

```
val Elim.f : KNormal.t -> KNormal.t

(* private *)
val Elim.effect : KNormal.t -> bool
```

After constant folding, we often find unused variable definitions (and unused function definitions) as in let $x = 3$ in let $y = 7$ in 10. MinCaml removes them in module Elim.

In general, if e_1 has no side effect and x does not appear free in e_2, we can replace let $x = e_1$ in e_2 just with e_2. The presence of side effects is checked by Elim.effect and the appearance of variables are examined by KNormal.fv. Since it is undecidable whether an expression has a real side effect, we treat any write to an array and any call to a function as side-effecting.

Mutually recursive functions defined by a single let rec are eliminated only when none of the functions is used in the continuation. If any of the functions are used after the definition, then all of them are kept.

4.10 Closure Conversion (136 Lines)

```
type Id.l (* label names *)
type Closure.t (* closure-converted expressions *)
type Closure.fundef =
  { name : Id.l * Type.t;
    args : (Id.t * Type.t) list;
    formal_fv : (Id.t * Type.t) list;
    body : Closure.t }
type Closure.prog =
    Prog of Closure.fundef list * Closure.t

val Closure.f : KNormal.t -> Closure.prog
val Closure.fv : Closure.t -> S.t

(* private *)
val Closure.toplevel : Closure.fundef list ref
val Closure.g : Type.t M.t (* typenv for fv *) ->
                S.t (* known functions *) ->
                KNormal.t -> Closure.t
```

Another gap still remaining between MinCaml and assembly is nested function definitions, which are flattened by closure conversion. It is the second most complicated process in our compiler. (The first is register allocation, which is described later.) What follows is how we explain closure conversion to students.

The flattening of nested function definitions includes easy cases and hard cases. For example,

```
let rec quad x =
  let rec dbl y = y + y in
  dbl (dbl x) in
quad 123
```

can be flattened like

```
let rec dbl y = y + y ;;
let rec quad x = dbl (dbl x) ;;
quad 123
```

just by moving the function definition. However, a similar manipulation would convert

```
let rec make_adder x =
  let rec adder y = x + y in
  adder in
(make_adder 3) 7
```

into

```
let rec adder y = x + y ;;
let rec make_adder x = adder ;;
(make_adder 3) 7
```

which makes no sense at all. This is because the function dbl has no free variable while adder has a free variable x.

Thus, in order to flatten function definitions with free variables, we have to treat not only the bodies of functions such as adder, but also the values of their free variables such as x together. In ML-like pseudo code, this treatment can be described as:

```
let rec adder x y = x + y ;;
let rec make_adder x = (adder, x) ;;
let (f, fv) = make_adder 3 in
f fv 7
```

First, function adder takes the value of its free variable x as an argument. Then, when the function is returned as a value, its body is paired with the value of its free variable. This pair is called a *function closure*. In general, when a function is called, its body and the values of its free variables are extracted from the closure and supplied as arguments.

The simple-minded approach of generating a closure for every function is too inefficient. Closure conversion gets more interesting when we try to separate the functions that require closures from those that can be called in more conventional ways. Thus, the closure conversion routine Closure.g of MinCaml takes the set known of functions that are statically known to have no free variables (and therefore can be called directly), and converts a given expression by using this information.

The results of closure conversion are represented in data type Closure.t that represents the following abstract syntax:

$P ::=$	
$\{D_1, \ldots, D_n\}, M$	whole program
$D ::=$	
$\ell(y_1, \ldots, y_m)(z_1, \ldots, z_n) = N$	top-level function definition
$M, N, e ::=$	
c	constants
$op(x_1, \ldots, x_n)$	arithmetic operations
if $x = y$ then M else N	conditional branches
if $x \leq y$ then M else N	conditional branches
let $x = M$ in N	variable definitions
x	variables
make_closure $x = (\ell, (z_1, \ldots, z_n))$ and ... in M	closure creation
apply_closure$(x, y_1, \ldots, y_n)$	closure-based function call
apply_direct$(\ell, y_1, \ldots, y_n)$	direct function call
$\vdots$	

It is similar to KNormal.t, but includes closure creation make_closure and top-level functions $D_1, \ldots, D_n$ instead of nested function definitions. In addition, instead of general function calls, it has closure-based function calls apply_closure and direct function calls apply_direct that do not use closures. Furthermore, in the processes that follow, we distinguish the type of top-level function names (labels) from the type of ordinary variable names in order to avoid confusions. Note that apply_closure uses variables while apply_direct uses labels. This is because closures are bound to variables (by make_closure) while top-level functions are called through labels.

Upon seeing a general function call $x\ y_1\ \ldots\ y_n$, Closure.g checks if the function x belongs to the set known. If so, it returns apply_direct. If not, it returns apply_closure.

```
| KNormal.App(x, ys) when S.mem x known ->
    AppDir(Id.L(x), ys)
| KNormal.App(f, xs) ->
    AppCls(f, xs)
```

Here, AppDir and AppCls are constructors in the Closure module that correspond to apply_direct and apply_closure, S is a module for sets, and Id.L is the constructor for labels.

Function definitions let rec $x\ y_1\ \ldots\ y_n = e_1$ in e_2 are processed as follows. First, we assume that the function x has no free variable, add it to known, and convert its body e_1. Then, if x indeed has no free variable, we continue the process and convert e_2. Otherwise, we rewind the values of known and toplevel (a reference cell holding top-level functions), and redo the conversion of e_1. (This may take exponential time with respect to the depth of nested function definitions, which is small in practice.) Finally, if x never appears as a proper variable (rather than a top-level label) in e_2, we omit the closure creation make_closure for function x.

This last optimization needs some elaboration. Even if x has no free variable, it may still need a representation as a closure, provided that it is returned as a value (consider, for example, let rec $x\ y = \ldots$ in x). This is because a user who receives x as a value does not know in general if it has a free variable or not, and therefore must anyway use apply_closure to call the function through its closure. In this case, we do not eliminate make_closure since x appears as a variable in e_2. However, if x is just called as a function, for example like let rec $x\ y = \ldots$ in x 123, then we eliminate the closure creation for x because it appears only as a label (not a variable) in apply_direct.

The closure conversion of mutually recursive functions is a little more complicated. In general, mutually recursive functions can share closures [5], but MinCaml does not implement this sharing. This simplifies the virtual machine code generation as discussed later. The drawback is that mutually recursive calls to functions with free variables get slower. However, we do *not* lose the efficiency of mutually recursive calls to functions with *no* free variables, because they are anyway converted to apply_direct.

4.11 Virtual Machine Code Generation (208 Lines)

```
type SparcAsm.t (* instruction sequences *)
type SparcAsm.exp (* atomic expressions *)
type SparcAsm.fundef =
  { name : Id.l;
    args : Id.t list; (* int arguments *)
    fargs : Id.t list; (* float arguments *)
    body : SparcAsm.t;
    ret : Type.t (* return type *)}
type SparcAsm.prog =
    Prog of (Id.l * float) list * (* float table *)
           SparcAsm.fundef list *
           SparcAsm.t

val SparcAsm.fv : SparcAsm.t -> Id.t list (* use order *)
val Virtual.f : Closure.prog -> SparcAsm.prog

(* private *)
val Virtual.data : (Id.l * float) list ref (* float table *)
val Virtual.h : Closure.fundef -> SparcAsm.fundef
val Virtual.g : Type.t M.t -> Closure.t -> SparcAsm.t
```

After closure conversion, we generate SPARC Assembly. Since it is too hard to output real assembly, we first generate *virtual* machine code similar to SPARC Assembly. Its main "virtual" aspects are:

- Infinite number of variables (instead of finite number of registers)
- if-then-else expressions and function calls (instead of comparisons, branches, and jumps)

This virtual assembly is defined in module SparcAsm. The ML data type SparcAsm.exp almost corresponds to each instruction of SPARC (except If and Call). Instruction sequences SparcAsm.t are either Ans, which returns a value at the end of a function, or a variable definition Let. The other instructions Forget, Save, and Restore will be explained later.

```
(* C(i) represents 13-bit immediates of SPARC *)
type id_or_imm = V of Id.t | C of int

type t =
  | Ans of exp
  | Let of (Id.t * Type.t) * exp * t
  | Forget of Id.t * t
and exp = (* excerpt *)
  | Set of int
  | SetL of Id.l
  | Add of Id.t * id_or_imm
  | Ld of Id.t * id_or_imm
  | St of Id.t * Id.t * id_or_imm
  | FAddD of Id.t * Id.t
  | LdDF of Id.t * id_or_imm
  | StDF of Id.t * Id.t * id_or_imm
  | IfEq of Id.t * id_or_imm * t * t
  | IfFEq of Id.t * Id.t * t * t
  | CallCls of Id.t * Id.t list * Id.t list
  | CallDir of Id.l * Id.t list * Id.t list
  | Save of Id.t * Id.t
  | Restore of Id.t
```

Virtual.f, Virtual.h, and Virtual.g are the three functions that translate closure-converted programs to virtual machine code. Virtual.f translates the whole program (the list of top-level functions and the expression of a main routine), Virtual.h translates each top-level function, and Virtual.g translates an expression. The point of these translations is to make explicit the memory accesses for creating, reading from, and writing to closures, tuples, and arrays. Data structures such as closures, tuples, and arrays are allocated in the heap, whose address is remembered in special register SparcAsm.reg_hp.

For example, to read from an array, we shift its offset according to the size of the element to be loaded.

```
| Closure.Get(x, y) ->
    let offset = Id.genid "o" in
    (match M.find x env with
    | Type.Array(Type.Unit) -> Ans(Nop)
    | Type.Array(Type.Float) ->
        Let((offset, Type.Int), SLL(y, C(3)),
            Ans(LdDF(x, V(offset))))
    | Type.Array(_) ->
        Let((offset, Type.Int), SLL(y, C(2)),
            Ans(Ld(x, V(offset))))
    | _ -> assert false)
```

In tuple creation Closure.Tuple, each element is stored with floating-point numbers aligned (in 8 bytes), and the starting address is used as the tuple's value. Closure creation Closure.MakeCls stores the address (label) of the function's body with the values of its free variables—also taking care of alignment—and uses the starting address as the closure's value. As mentioned in the previous section, this is easy because we generate separate closures with no sharing at all even for mutually recursive functions. Accordingly, at the beginning of each top-level function, we load the values of free variables from the closure, where every closure-based function application (AppCls) is assumed to set the closure's address to register SparcAsm.reg_cl.

In addition, since SPARC Assembly does not support floating-point immediates, we need to create a constant table in memory. For this purpose, Virtual.g records floating-point constants to global variable Virtual.data.

4.12 13-Bit Immediate Optimization (42 Lines)

```
val Simm13.f : SparcAsm.prog -> SparcAsm.prog
```

In SPARC Assembly, most integer operations can take an immediate within 13 bits (no less than -4096 and less than 4096) as the second operand. An optimization using this feature is implemented in module Simm13. It is almost the same as constant folding and elimination of unnecessary definitions, except that the object language is virtual assembly and the constants are limited to 13-bit integers.

4.13 Register Allocation (262 Lines)

```
val RegAlloc.f : SparcAsm.prog -> SparcAsm.prog

(* private *)
type g_result =
   NoSpill of SparcAsm.t * Id.t M.t
 | ToSpill of SparcAsm.t * Id.t list
val RegAlloc.h : SparcAsm.fundef -> SparcAsm.fundef
val RegAlloc.g : Id.t * Type.t (* dest *) ->
                 SparcAsm.t (* cont *) ->
                 Id.t M.t (* regenv *) ->
                 SparcAsm.t -> g_result
val RegAlloc.g' : Id.t * Type.t (* dest *) ->
                  SparcAsm.t (* cont *) ->
                  Id.t M.t (* regenv *) ->
                  SparcAsm.exp -> g_result
```

The most complex process in The MinCaml Compiler is register allocation, which implements infinite number of variables by finite number of registers. As discussed in Section 3, our register allocator adopts a greedy algorithm with backtracking for early spilling and look-ahead for register targeting.

4.13.1 Basics

First of all, as a function calling convention, we will assign arguments from the first register toward the last register. (Our compiler does not support too many arguments that do not fit in registers. They must be handled by programmers, for example by using tuples.) We set return values to the first register. These are processed in RegAlloc.h, which allocates registers in each top-level function.

After that, we allocate registers in function bodies and the main routine. RegAlloc.g takes an instruction sequence with a mapping regenv from variables to registers that represents the current register assignment, and returns the instruction sequence after register allocation. The basic policy of register allocation is to avoid registers already assigned to live variables. The set of live variables are calculated by SparcAsm.fv.

However, when allocating registers in the instruction sequence e_1 of let $x = e_1$ in e_2, not only e_1 but also its "continuation" e_2 must be taken into account for the calculation of live variables. For this reason, RegAlloc.g and RegAlloc.g', which allocates registers in individual instructions, also take the continuation instruction sequence cont and use it in the calculation of live variables.

4.13.2 Spilling

We sometimes cannot allocate any register that is not live, since the number of variables is infinite while that of registers is not. In this case, we have to save the value of some register to memory. This process is called register spilling. Unlike in imperative languages, the value of a variable in functional languages does not change after its definition. Therefore, it is better to save the value of a variable *as early as possible*, if at all, in order to make the room.

Whenever a variable x needs to be saved, RegAlloc.g returns a value ToSpill, and returns to the definition of x to insert a virtual instruction Save. In addition, since we want to remove x from the set of live variables at the point where x is spilled, we insert another virtual instruction Forget to exclude x from the set of free variables. For this purpose, value ToSpill carries not only the list xs of spilled variables, but also the instruction sequence e in which Forget has been inserted. After saving x, we redo the register allocation against e.

Saving is necessary not only when registers are spilled, but also when functions are called. MinCaml adopts the caller-save convention, so every function call is assumed to destroy the values of all registers. Therefore, we need to save the values of all registers that are live at that point, as implemented in an auxiliary function RegAlloc.g'_call. This is why ToSpill holds the *list* of spilled variables.

When saving is unnecessary, we return the register-allocated instruction sequence e' (with the new regenv) in another value NoSpill.

To put it altogether, the data type for the returned values of these functions is defined as follows:

```
type g_result =
    NoSpill of
        SparcAsm.t (* instruction sequence
                      with registers allocated *)
      * Id.t M.t   (* new regenv *)
  | ToSpill of
        SparcAsm.t (* instruction sequence
                      with Forget inserted *)
      * Id.t list  (* spilled variables *)
```

4.13.3 Unspilling

A spilled variable will be used sooner or later, in which case RegAlloc.g' (the function that allocates registers in individual instructions) raises an exception as it cannot find the variable in regenv. This exception is handled in an auxiliary function RegAlloc.g'_and_unspill, where virtual instruction Restore is inserted to restore the value of the variable from memory to a register.

However, this insertion of Restore pseudo-instructions breaks a fundamental property of our virtual assembly that every variable is assigned just one register. In particular, it leads to a discrepancy when two flows of a program join after conditional branches. For example, in the then-clause of expression (if $f()$ then $x - y$ else $y - x$) $+ x + y$, variable x may be restored into register r_0 and y may be restored into r_1, while they may be restored in the other order in the else-clause. (A similar discrepancy also arises concerning whether a variable is spilled or not.)

In imperative languages, such "discrepancies" are so common that a more sophisticated notion of *def-use chains* is introduced and used as the unit of register allocation (instead of individual variables). In MinCaml, fortunately, those cases are less common and can be treated in a simpler manner: whenever a variable is not in the same register after conditional branches, it is just assumed as spilled (and needs to be restored before being used again), as implemented in an auxiliary function RegAlloc.g'_if.

4.13.4 Targeting

When allocating registers, we not only avoid live registers, but also try to reduce unnecessary moves in the future. This is called register targeting [5], itself an instance of register coalescing [18]. For example, if a variable being defined will be the second argument of a function call, we try to allocate it on the second register. For another example, we try to allocate a variable on the first register if it will be returned as the result of a function. These are implemented in RegAlloc.target. For this purpose, RegAlloc.g and RegAlloc.g' also takes register dest as an argument, where the result of computation will be stored.

4.13.5 Summary

All in all, the main functions in module RegAlloc can be described as follows.

RegAlloc.g dest cont regenv e allocates registers in instruction sequence e. It takes into account the continuation instruction sequence cont when calculating live variables. Already allocated variables in e are substituted with registers according to the mapping regenv. The value computed by e is stored to dest.

RegAlloc.g' is similar to RegAlloc.g but takes individual instructions (SparcAsm.exp) instead of instruction sequences (SparcAsm.t). However, it still *returns* instruction sequences—not individual instructions—so that spilling and unspilling can be inserted. It uses auxiliary functions RegAlloc.g'_call and RegAlloc.g'_if to deal with spilling due to function calls and conditional branches, while unspilling is treated by another auxiliary function RegAlloc.g'_and_unspill.

All of the functions above return either NoSpill(e', regenv2) or ToSpill(e, xs). The former means that register allocation has succeeded: regenv2 is the new mapping from variables to registers, and e' is the instruction sequence where all variables have been substituted with the allocated registers. The latter means that register spilling is required: xs is the list of spilled variables, and e is the instruction sequence where Forget pseudo-instructions have been inserted. Both results must be treated by every caller of RegAlloc.g or RegAlloc.g'.

Finally, RegAlloc.h takes a top-level function definition and allocates registers. RegAlloc.f takes a whole program and allocates registers. Actually, it is the only function exported by module RegAlloc.

4.14 Assembly Generation (256 Lines)

```
val Emit.f : ochan -> SparcAsm.prog -> unit

(* private *)
type dest = Tail | NonTail of Id.t
val Emit.h : ochan -> SparcAsm.fundef -> unit
val Emit.g : ochan -> dest * SparcAsm.t -> unit
val Emit.g' : ochan -> dest * SparcAsm.exp -> unit
```

At last, we reach the final phase: assembly generation. Having done most of the hard work (register allocation, in particular), it is easy to output SparcAsm.t as real SPARC Assembly by replacing virtual instructions with real ones. Conditional expressions are implemented by comparisons and branches. Save and Restore are implemented with stores and loads by calculating the set stackset of already saved variables (to avoid redundant saves) and the list stackmap of their locations in the stack. Function calls are a little trickier: Emit.shuffle is used to potentially re-arrange arguments in register order.

```
(* given a list (xys) of parallel moves,
   implements it by sequential moves
   using a temporary register (tmp) *)
let rec shuffle tmp xys =
  (* remove identical moves *)
  let _, xys =
    List.partition (fun (x, y) -> x = y) xys in
  (* find acyclic moves *)
  match (List.partition
           (fun (_, y) -> List.mem_assoc y xys)
           xys) with
  | [], [] -> []
  | (x, y) :: xys, [] ->
      (* no acyclic moves; resolve a cyclic move *)
      (y, tmp) :: (x, y) ::
      shuffle tmp
        (List.map
           (function
             | (x', y') when x' = y -> (tmp, y')
             | xy -> xy)
           xys)
  | xys, acyc -> acyc @ shuffle tmp xys
```

Tail calls are detected and optimized in this module. For this purpose, function Emit.g (which generates assembly for instruction sequences) as well as function Emit.g' (which generates assembly for individual instructions) takes a value of data type Emit.dest that represents whether we are in a tail position:

```
type dest = Tail | NonTail of Id.t
```

If this value is Tail, we tail-call another function by a jump instruction, or set the result of computation to the first register and return by the ret instruction of SPARC. If it is NonTail(x), the result of computation is stored in x.

4.15 Main Routine, Auxiliary Modules, and Runtime Library (45 + 228 + 197 Lines)

After parsing command-line arguments, the main routine of MinCaml applies all the processes above. It also repeats the five optimizations from β-reduction to elimination of unnecessary definitions until their result reaches a fixed point (or the number of iterations reaches the maximum specified by a user).

Finally, we provide a few auxiliary modules, write the runtime routine stub.c which allocates the heap and stack of MinCaml, implement external functions libmincaml.s in SPARC Assembly for I/O and math, and obtain The MinCaml Compiler.

5. Efficiency

The main point of MinCaml was to let students understand how functional programs can be compiled into efficient code. So we had to demonstrate the efficiency of the code generated by MinCaml. For this purpose, we implemented several applications and compiled them with MinCaml, Objective Caml, and GCC. Each program was written in the optimal style of each language implementation, so that the compiler produces as fast code as possible (to the best of our knowledge) without changing the essential algorithms. These comparisons are never meant to be "fair," in the sense that MinCaml supports only a tiny language—in fact, it is *intended* to be minimal—while other compilers support real languages. Rather, they must be understood as informal references.

First, as small benchmarks, we chose three typical functional programs: Ackermann, Fibonacci, and Takeuchi (also known as Tak) functions. The first two of them test recursion on integers, and the last on floating-point numbers. The results are shown in Table 3. All the numbers are user-level execution times in seconds, measured by `/usr/bin/time`.

The machine is Sun Fire V880 (4 Ultra SPARC III 1.2GHz, 8GB main memory, Solaris 9). MinCaml is given the option `-inline 100`, meaning to inline functions whose size (the number of syntactic nodes in K-normal forms) is less than 100. OCamlOpt is version 3.08.3 and given the options `-unsafe -inline 100`. GCC `-m32` and GCC `-m64` are version 4.0.0 20050319 and given the option `-O3`. GCC `-m32 -mflat` is version 3.4.3 (since more recent versions do not support `-mflat`) and given the same option `-O3`. Note that GCC4 (and, to a lesser degree, GCC3) often produces faster code than older versions such as GCC2.

Although small benchmarks typically suffer from subtle effects of low-level mechanisms in a particular processor—such caches, alignments, and pipelines—our programs did not: indeed, looking at the assembly generated by each compiler, we found more obvious reasons for our results:

- Objective Caml and GCC3 do not inline recursive functions, while MinCaml and GCC4 do.
- Objective Caml boxes—i.e., allocates in the heap—floating-point numbers passed as arguments (or returned as results) of functions in order to support polymorphism, though it does support unboxed *arrays* (and records) of floating-point numbers.
- GCC without `-mflat` (both `-m32` and `-m64`) uses the register window mechanism of SPARC, which is almost always less efficient than other function calling conventions because it saves (and restores) *all* registers including unused ones.
- GCC with `-mflat` uses a callee-save convention instead of register windows, which is still suboptimal since it only saves registers in the prologues of functions (and restores them in their epilogues), not in the middle of them.
- GCC4 reduces arithmetic expressions such as $(n-1)-2$, which appears after the inlining of Fibonacci, to $n-3$.
- GCC `-m32` (with or without `-mflat`) passes floating-point number function arguments through integer registers, which incurs an overhead.

Second, we tested larger applications: ray tracing, a harmonic function, the Mandelbrot set, and Huffman encoding. All of them are first written in C and then ported to ML. In Objective Caml, we adopted an imperative style with references and `for`-statements whenever it is faster than a function style. However, we always used tail recursion in MinCaml, since it does not have any other loop construct. The results are also in Table 3. Again, Objective Caml tends to be slower than other compiles because of boxing when floating-point numbers are used as arguments of functions or elements of tuples (which cannot be replaced with arrays because they contain other types of elements as well). MinCaml also tends to be a little slower than GCC because loops are implemented by tail recursive functions, and entering to (or leaving from) them requires extra saves (or restores) of variables not used within the loops. In addition, GCC implements instruction scheduling for floating-point operations in order to hide their latencies, while MinCaml does not.

	MinCaml	OCamlOpt `-unsafe`	GCC4 `-m32`	GCC4 `-m64`	GCC3 `-m32 -mflat`
Ackermann	0.3	0.3	1.3	1.8	1.0
Fibonacci	2.5	3.9	1.5	1.4	6.1
Takeuchi	1.6	3.8	3.7	1.6	5.5
Ray Tracing	3.4	7.5	2.3	2.9	2.6
Harmonic	2.6	2.6	2.0	2.0	2.0
Mandelbrot	1.8	4.6	1.7	1.7	1.5
Huffman	4.5	6.6	2.8	3.0	2.9

Table 3. Execution Time of Benchmark Programs

To summarize, for these modest benchmarks that can be written in our minimal language, the efficiency of MinCaml is comparable to major compilers such as Objective Caml and GCC with the speed ratio varying from "6 times faster" at best to "twice slower" at worst.

6. Related Work

There exist many compilers for ML and its variants: Comp.Lang.ML FAQ [1] gives a comprehensive list. However, I am not aware of any publicly available compiler that is as simple and efficient as MinCaml. There also exist various textbooks and tutorials on compilation of functional languages, but most of them present compilers into byte code or other medium-level languages—not native assembly—which do not satisfy our requirement for efficiency. The only exception that I am aware of is a well-known book by Appel [5], which uses CPS as the intermediate language and is distinct from MinCaml as argued below.

Hilsdale et al. [14] presented a compiler for a subset of Scheme, implemented in Scheme, that generates native assembly. However, efficiency of the generated code is not discussed at all, perhaps because it was not a goal in their compiler.

Sarkar et al. [23] developed a compiler course (using Scheme) based on the *nanopass* framework, where the compiler consists of many small translation (or verification) processes written in a domain specific language developed for this purpose. Unlike nanopass, we chose to use ordinary ML as the meta language in order to avoid the overhead of understanding such a domain specific language itself, and to utilize the type system of ML for statically checking the syntactic validity of intermediate code even *before* running the compiler.

Feeley [10] presented a Scheme-to-C compiler which is supposed to be explained in "90 minutes" and implemented in less than 800 lines of Scheme. Its main focuses are on CPS conversion and closure conversion for first-class continuations and higher-order functions. Optimizations are out of scope: indeed, the compiler is reported to produce 6 times slower code than Gambit-C does. By contrast, our compiler is a little more complex but much more efficient.

Dijkstra and Swierstra [9] are developing a compiler for Haskell based on attribute grammar. It is presented as a sequence of implementations with increasing complexities. So far, their main focus seems to be on typing. To the best of my knowledge, little code or no documentation is available for compilation at this moment. In addition, the most complex version of their compiler is already about 10,000 lines long, excluding an implementation of their domain specific language based on attribute grammar.[3]

One [6] of Appel's series of textbooks implements a compiler *of* an imperative language (called Tiger) *in* ML. This language is not primarily functional and is fundamentally different from ML. For instance, higher-order functions and type inference are only optional [6, Chapters 15 and 16]. With those options, the compiler is much more complex than ours.

MinCaml adopts a variant of K-normal forms [7] as an intermediate language, which itself is a variant of A-normal forms [11]. Another major intermediate language of functional language compilers is continuation passing style (CPS) [5]. The crucial difference between K-normal forms and CPS, which lead us to choose the former, is conditional branches in non-tail positions: since all conditional branches must be in tail positions in CPS, non-tail branches are converted to tail branches with closure creations and function applications, which incur overheads and require optimizations (such as the so-called "callee-save" registers or inter-procedural register allocation).

On the other hand, however, CPS compiles function calls in a very elegant way without *a priori* assuming the notion of call stacks. Besides, K-normal forms have their own complication—which in essence stems from the same root—with non-tail branches (cf. the second and third paragraphs of Section 4.13.3) and, to a lesser degree, `let`-expressions (cf. the last paragraph of Section 4.13.1). Thus, it would also be interesting to see how simple and efficient compiler for education can be developed by using CPS instead of `let`-based intermediate languages.

As we saw in Section 4.13, the most complex process in The MinCaml Compiler was register allocation. Although there exist more standard methods than ours such as graph coloring [8] and linear scan [21], we find them less clear (though much faster at compile-time) in the context of functional languages, in particular concerning where and how to insert spilling and unspilling.

7. Conclusion

We presented an educational compiler, written in 2000 lines of ML, for a minimal functional language. For several applications that can be written in this language, we showed that our compiler produces assembly code of comparable efficiency to Objective Caml and GCC.

The use of MinCaml in Tokyo has been successful. Most of the groups accomplished the implementation of compilers and ran ray tracing on their CPUs. Some students liked ML so much that they started a portal site (`http://www.ocaml.jp/`) and a mailing list as well as a translation of the manual of Objective Caml, all in Japanese.

Like many program transformations in functional languages, most processes in our compiler are implemented by tree traversal over abstract syntax and have many similarities to one another. For instance, functions `KNormal.fv` and `Closure.fv` are almost identical except for the necessary differences such as `let rec` and `make_closure`. This kind of similarities could perhaps be exploited to simplify the compiler even more through subtyping (by means of polymorphic variants [13], for example) or generic programming in the style of Generic Haskell (`http://www.generic-haskell.org/`).

Although our language was designed to be minimal, its extensions would be useful for more advanced—maybe graduate—courses, and perhaps as a vehicle for research prototypes. Features required for these purposes include polymorphism, data types, pattern matching, garbage collection, and modules. We are looking into the tradeoff between simplicity and efficiency of various methods for implementing them.

We chose SPARC Assembly as our target code because of its simplicity and availability in Tokyo, but re-targeting to IA-32 would also be interesting from the viewpoint of popularization in spite of the more complex instruction set architecture. We are also looking into this direction—in particular, how to adapt our code generator to 2-operand instructions (which are destructive by definition) in a "functional" way.

Acknowledgments

I would like to thank Dr. Yutaka Oiwa for porting the ray tracer to MinCaml. Prof. Kenichi Asai, Prof. Kazuhiko Kato, Prof. Kenjiro Taura, and Dr. Yoshihiro Oyama gave useful comments and suggestions, encouraging this project.

References

[1] Comp.lang.ml FAQ. `http://www.faqs.org/faqs/meta-lang-faq/`.

[2] The computer language shootout benchmarks. `http://shootout.alioth.debian.org/`.

[3] ICFP programming contest. `http://icfpcontest.org/`.

[4] MLton Standard ML compiler. `http://mlton.org/`.

[5] A. W. Appel. *Compiling with Continuations*. Cambridge University Press, 1992.

[6] A. W. Appel. *Modern Compiler Implementation in ML*. Cambridge University Press, 1998.

[7] L. Birkedal, M. Tofte, and M. Vejlstrup. From region inference to von neumann machines via region representation inference. In *Proceedings of the 23rd ACM SIGPLAN-SIGACT Symposium on Principles of Programming Languages*, pages 171–183, 1996.

[8] G. J. Chaitin. Register allocation & spilling via graph coloring. In *Proceedings of the 1982 SIGPLAN Symposium on Compiler Construction*, pages 98–101, 1982.

[9] A. Dijkstra and S. D. Swierstra. Essential Haskell compiler. `http://catamaran.labs.cs.uu.nl/twiki/st/bin/view/Ehc/WebHome`.

[10] M. Feeley. The 90 minute Scheme to C compiler. `http://www.iro.umontreal.ca/~boucherd/mslug/meetings/20041020/`.

[11] C. Flanagan, A. Sabry, B. F. Duba, and M. Felleisen. The essence of compiling with continuations. In *Proceedings of the ACM SIGPLAN '93 Conference on Programming Language Design and Implementation*, pages 237–247, 1993. In *ACM SIGPLAN Notices*, 28(6), June 1993.

[12] B. Ford. Packrat parsing: Simple, powerful, lazy, linear time. In *Proceedings of the Seventh ACM SIGPLAN International Conference on Functional Programming*, pages 36–47, 2002.

[13] J. Garrigue. Programming with polymorphic variants. In *Proceedings of the 1998 ACM SIGPLAN Workshop on ML*, 1998.

[14] E. Hilsdale, J. M. Ashley, R. K. Dybvig, and D. P. Friedman. Compiler construction using Scheme. In *Functional Programming Languages in Education*, volume 1022 of *Lecture Notes in Computer Science*, pages 251–267. Springer-Verlag, 1995.

[15] T. Jim. What are principal typings and what are they good for? In *Proceedings of the 23rd ACM SIGPLAN-SIGACT Symposium on Principles of Programming Languages*, pages 42–53, 1996.

[16] J. L. Lawall and O. Danvy. Continuation-based partial evaluation. In *Proceedings of the 1994 ACM Conference on LISP and Functional Programming*, volume VII of *ACM SIGPLAN Lisp Pointers*, pages 227–238, 1994.

[17] Y. Minamide, G. Morrisett, and R. Harper. Typed closure conversion. In *Proceedings of the 23rd ACM SIGPLAN-SIGACT Symposium on Principles of Programming Languages*, pages 271–283, 1996.

[18] S. Muchnick. *Advanced Compiler Design and Implementation*. Morgan Kaufmann, 1997.

[19] A. Ohori. A polymorphic record calculus and its compilation. *ACM Transactions on Programming Languages and Systems*, 17(6):844–895, 1995.

[20] S. Peyton Jones and S. Marlow. Secrets of the Glasgow Haskell Compiler inliner. *Journal of Functional Programming*, 12(4):393–434, 2002.

[21] M. Poletto and V. Sarkar. Linear scan register allocation. *ACM Transactions on Programming Languages and Systems*, 21(5):895–913, 1999.

[22] D. Rémy. Type inference for records in a natural extension of ML. In C. A. Gunter and J. C. Mitchell, editors, *Theoretical Aspects of Object-Oriented Programming: Types, Semantics, and Language Design*. MIT Press, 1994.

[23] D. Sarkar, O. Waddell, and R. K. Dybvig. A nanopass infrastructure for compiler education. In *Proceedings of the Ninth ACM SIGPLAN International Conference on Functional Programming*, pages 201 – 212, 2004.

[24] P. Wadler. Why no one uses functional languages. *SIGPLAN Notices*, 33(8):23–27, 1998.

[3] Of course, line numbers are not always an exact measure of software complexity—in particular for different languages—but they often approximate it with a certain precision.

Engineering Software Correctness

Rex Page
University of Oklahoma
School of Computer Science
Norman OK USA
1 405 325 5048
page@ou.edu

ABSTRACT

Software engineering courses offer one of many opportunities for providing students with a significant experience in declarative programming. This report discusses some results from taking advantage of this opportunity in a two-semester sequence of software engineering courses for students in their final year of baccalaureate studies in computer science. The sequence is based on functional programming using ACL2, a purely functional subset of Common Lisp with a built-in, computational logic developed by J Strother Moore and his colleagues over the past three decades. The course sequence has been offered twice, so far, in two consecutive academic years. Certain improvements evolved in the second offering, and while this report focuses on that offering, it also offers reasons for the changes. The discussion outlines the topical coverage and required projects, suggests further improvements, and observes educational effects based on conversations with students and evaluations of their course projects. In general, it appears that most students enjoyed the approach and learned concepts and practices of interest to them. Seventy-six students have completed the two-course sequence, half of them in the first offering and half in the second. All of the students gained enough competence in functional programming to apply it in future projects in industry or graduate school. In the second offering, about forty percent of the students gained enough competence with the ACL2 mechanized logic to make significant use of it in verifying properties of software. About ten percent acquired more competence than might reasonably be expected, enough to see new opportunities for applications and lead future software development efforts in the direction of declarative software with proven correctness properties.

Categories and Subject Descriptors K.3.2 [**Computer and Information Science Education**]: *Computer science education, Curriculum.*
D.1.1 [**Applicative (Functional) Programming**]

D.2.4 [**Software/Program Verification**]: Correctness proofs, Formal methods.

General Terms Design, Languages, Verification.

Keywords Software engineering education, functional programming, Lisp, ACL2, mechanized logic, theorem provers

1. OPPORTUNITIES

Software engineering courses offer one of many opportunities for providing students with a significant experience in declarative programming. Many computer science programs require at least one course in software engineering, and some require more.

For example, the technical portion of the baccalaureate curriculum in computer science at the University of Oklahoma comprises seventy-three credit-hours of coursework. (One credit-hour is awarded for one fifty-minute lecture per week for a sixteen-week semester.) The seventy-three credits-hours are parceled into twenty-three, three-credit courses and one four-credit course. Half of these are mathematics courses (four of which — applied logic, discrete mathematics, theory of computation, and algorithm analysis — are taught by the School of Computer Science). The other half are engineering courses (all of which are taught by the School of Computer Science). Eight of the twelve computer science courses (or more, depending on electives) involve significant software or hardware development.

None of the courses with significant software development assignments prescribe any particular technology in their official descriptions, but by agreement of the faculty, the first three courses (introduction to computer programming, programming structures and abstractions, and data structures) use Java and C++ to describe computations. The other courses leave to the instructor and/or the student the choice of programming languages and other software development tools.

Before 2003, no course in the curriculum afforded students a significant experience in declarative programming. Sometimes students in the programming language course wrote short programs in a functional language such as Scheme or in a logic language such as Prolog. However, these ten- to twenty-line programs could in no way provide students with enough background to apply declarative programming to future projects. Substantial additional education would be required to meet that goal, and the curriculum did not provide an opportunity to get that education.

In 2003, I began using declarative programming in a two-course sequence in software engineering: Software Engineering I and Software Engineering II. The remainder of this report discusses this experiment and some of the results.

2. READING GUIDE

The following summary of topics may serve as a reading guide:

Section 3. Evolution of the courses

Section 4. Overview of first semester (SE-I)

Section 5. Software verification examples from lectures

Section 6. Projects from first semester

Section 7. Overview of second semester (SE-II)

Section 8. Projects from second semester

Section 9. Student reactions and accomplishments

Section 10. Changes that might be desirable

Section 11. Conjectures about potential benefits

Section 12. Downloading course materials

3. HISTORY

All baccalaureate students in our computer science program are required to take a two-course sequence (six credit-hours in all) in software engineering. Almost all of them take this sequence during the last year of their studies.

The official description of the first of these courses, Software Engineering I, is "Methods and tools for software specification, design, and documentation. Emphasis on architectural modularity, encapsulation of software objects, and software development processes such as design review, code inspection, and defect tracking. Students working in teams apply these ideas to design and document software products. Study of professional ethics, responsibility, and liability." The course catalog has the following description for Software Engineering II: "Methods and tools for software development, testing, and delivery. Emphasis on data abstraction and reusable components. Students working in teams implement a significant software product, including design documents, user's guide, and process reports, using methods and processes studied in Software Engineering I. Students will practice oral and written communication skills."

As taught (by me, as least), the courses have three primary elements: design, software development processes, and defect control. Students work in teams in both courses. Software Engineering I places more weight on individual work than on team projects, while Software Engineering II gives teamwork more weight.

There are many ways to put together educational material on design, software processes, and defect control. Accordingly, in the six academic years in which I have taught the two-course sequence in software engineering, I have put the material together in several different ways.

In the beginning I based the course on traditional textbooks, such as Pressman [5] or Sommerville [6] and supplemented the material with experiences from industry. These textbooks cover a great deal of ground, but in a way that I find unsatisfying. There is little material of intellectual depth, and the books are entirely noncommittal on software engineering methods. One way is as good as another. Well … maybe some ways are better suited for some applications and other ways for other applications, but the authors provide no useful information about how to choose. Students are encouraged to learn a litany of terms and techniques, but without much motivation to go to the trouble.

Later, I began to use a textbook by Humphrey [2], which emphasizes software processes, and supplemented it with material on design and implementation. The book covers less ground than the traditional textbooks, and it does a poor job in covering software design, but it provides excellent coverage of software processes, and in a form that makes it practical for students to experience some of the benefits of applying such processes. The material is especially attentive to defect control in software development. Processes are experienced by students in the form of a specific set of estimation and record-keeping activities that Humphrey calls the Personal Software Process (PSP). It is presented with about as much intellectual depth as is possible for software process coverage, and the book takes a specific, useful point of view about software development.

During all of this period (pre-Humphrey and post-Humphrey) Software Engineering I was organized around six to ten small software development projects carried out by individual students, and Software Engineering II was organized around one, medium-sized project (5,000 to 15,000 lines of code) carried out by teams of four to six students. Students implemented software in a variety of languages (C++ and Java primarily, sometimes supplemented by scripting languages such as Tcl/Tk, Microsoft Word macros, or HTML managers). In every case, programming followed a conventional (that is, stateful) paradigm.

Two years ago, I decided to try using a declarative paradigm to boost the design and defect-control elements in the course. During the 2003-2004 academic year, the students used Scheme (specifically, the DrScheme environment [1] with its associated user interface tools) to implement their software, but wrote computational functions (as distinguished from functions performing some sort of input or output) in ACL2 [3], a purely functional subset of Common Lisp with a computational logic (theorem prover) for verifying properties of defined functions. This made it possible for students to verify, by way of mathematical proof, certain properties of the software they were writing. They used a mechanical translator to convert the functions they had defined in ACL2 to Scheme, to integrate them with their i/o-performing functions.

The main problem with this approach was that it failed to give most students a really significant exposure to functional programming methods. Most students expanded their i/o-performing functions in every way they could think of. Then, they could avoid functional programming in most of their code and use conventional methods for the bulk of it. Discouraging this tendency to minimize the portion of the program written in functional form, whether through grading or through discussions with individual students, proved to be impossible (for me) without seeming arbitrary or unreasonable.

Based on this experience, I required the students to write all code in ACL2 in the 2004-2005 academic year. This made all of the code conform to the purely functional paradigm and gave the students a consummate experience in functional programming. The primary disadvantage was that the assigned problems had to be designed to avoid interactive input/output operations, since those would be clumsy, at best, in ACL2. A secondary disadvantage, compared with Scheme, was the lack of higher-order functions in the ACL2 subset of Common Lisp. Neither of these disadvantages turned out to cause any significant problems, and the advantage to the students of experiencing the benefits of functional programming easily outweighed the disadvantages.

The remainder of this report focuses on the 2004-2005 offering of Software Engineering I and II, with the all-ACL2 requirement.

4. SE-I

The 2004 edition of Software Engineering I required each student to complete six small software development projects (100 to 500 lines each) working alone. The course also required students working in teams to complete one software development project of modest size (about 1,500 lines of code, including some reused code from the individual projects) and to cooperate in a prescribed way in the development of a smaller piece of software earlier in the course. I formed the teams (five or six students per team) with a view to balancing the talent and following other criteria developed by Larry Michaelson in his work on team-based learning [4].

Each individual software development project in Software Engineering I requires the students to deliver four items: design, code, PSP report [2], and proven theorems. The design is presented as a boxes-and-arrows chart, together with some textual descriptions of data structures, interfaces, and algorithmic decisions. The code is written entirely in ACL2. The Humphrey-style, PSP report includes a project plan, a software size estimate using a statistical estimation method based on historical data (estimates get better as the course progresses), a time log, a defect log, and a collection of test designs and reports.

Theorems (stated in ACL2 logic) express properties of functions written for the project. In the individual projects, specific theorems are given in the project assignment, to keep the students from floundering around with things they are unlikely to be able to get ACL2 to prove. In the first couple of problems, these theorems, once correctly stated in ACL2 logic, are things that the computational logic of ACL2 can prove without special hints.

As the course progresses, the project assignments specify theorems that require students to find additional supporting lemmas that ACL2 can prove directly. After ACL2 has the supporting lemmas in its database, it can proceed successfully to prove the target theorems.

This approach (stating theorems, finding that ACL2 cannot prove them on its own, discovering lemmas that ACL2 can prove and that provide a basis for proving other theorems, and finally working up to successful proofs of the originally stated theorems) is part of what the authors of the ACL2 book [3] call "The Method." It is one of many techniques that users of ACL2 must master to succeed in verifying significant software properties. It is the primary theorem-proving technique emphasized in the course.

The team software projects have the same four deliverables, and size estimates are based on averages of individual PSP data [2]. Altogether there are seven team projects in the course (five of which primarily concern software process issues) and seven individual projects (six of which are software development).

Twenty-one of the thirty-one, seventy-five-minute, class periods in Software Engineering I are devoted to lectures, and the remaining ten class periods are used as meeting-time by the teams to work on team projects. Five lectures address primarily design issues, eight focus on ACL2 (both as a programming language and as a computational logic), and six concern software processes.

5. LECTURES ON ACL2

Lectures on ACL2 in the first semester (SE-I) have three themes: (1) defining functions in the form of equations expressed in Lisp (the first experience with declarative programming for many of the students), (2) specifying properties of functions in the logic of ACL2, and (3) getting the ACL2 theorem prover to verify the properties, sometimes by supplementing with lemmas and building gradually to proofs of the desired properties.

The first lectures on ACL2 discuss non-recursive functions from propositional logic and theorems with non-inductive proofs, such as de Morgan's laws. I go through the proofs by hand, and then demonstrate that ACL2 succeeds in mechanizing them.

```
(defthm take-append-identity
  (implies (true-listp xs)
           (equal (take (length xs) (append xs ys)) xs)))
(defthm drop-append-identity
  (implies (true-listp xs)
           (equal (drop (length xs) (append xs ys)) ys)))
```

Figure 1. Correctness of concatenation.

Inductive examples come next, starting with the associativity of concatenation, the canonical example of the Boyer-Moore theorem prover from which ACL2 evolved. Most theorems discussed in the lectures relate directly to correctness, as in the relationships between the take, drop, length, and concatenation operations (Figure 1) that confirm the correctness of concatenation (assuming the correctness of the other operations).

Another early inductive example has to do with conservation of atomic elements in a function that flattens a tree (Figure 2).

```
(defun flatten (tr)
  (if (atom tr)
      (cons tr nil)
      (append (flatten (car tr)) (flatten (cdr tr)))))
(defun occurs-in (x tr)
  (or (and (atom x) (atom tr) (equal x tr))
      (and (atom x)
           (not (atom tr))
           (or (occurs-in x (car tr))
               (occurs-in x (cdr tr))))))
(defthm flatten-conserves-atoms
  (iff (occurs-in x tr)
       (and (atom x) (member x (flatten tr)))))
```

Figure 2. Flatten conserves atoms.

ACL2 proves all of these early theorems directly from their statements. When numbers are involved, it needs a little help from some arithmetic theorems supplied with ACL2, but no special steps are required. In these examples, one simply states the correctness properties, and the rest is automatic. However, it's not entirely trivial to state the theorems correctly. For example, without the true-list predicate (specifying a nil-terminated list) in the hypothesis of either theorem on concatenation (Figure 2), the equality in the conclusion may fail.

This is consistent with programming experience. What is true for the test-and-debug approach to software development is also true for a regimen that includes mechanically verified software properties: Initial expectations of a piece of software often turn out to be wrong. Knowing the conditions under which a formula delivers the intended result makes software more reliable, and that is one kind of information provided by software properties verified through computational logic.

```
(defun drop (n xs)
  (if (or (<= n 0) (atom xs))
      xs
      (drop (– n 1) (cdr xs))))
```

Figure 3. Incorrect definition of drop.

One lecture is devoted to defining the drop function, getting ACL2 to admit it to its logic (that is, to prove that it terminates), and verifying some of its properties. A naïve definition (Figure 3) fails to specify that the numeric argument must be integral, and an examination of ACL2's attempt at a termination proof shows that it runs off track trying to deal with the possibility that the number might be complex. ACL2 is able to complete the proof when the argument is constrained to integral values.

For both inductive and non-inductive theorems, the lectures present informal proofs, at the level of normal, mathematical argumentation, and point out that these informal proofs gloss over thousands of details that are not overlooked by the mechanized logic of ACL2. Part of the point is that informal proofs of software properties have limited value because they are at least as likely to be defective as function definitions. It is only with full mechanization that software verification has real value.

In more advanced examples, it is necessary to derive several lemmas from the steps in an informal proof to lead ACL2 to a successful proof ("The Method" [3]). One such example is a function that parcels a list into packets. Each packet is a contiguous sublist of the original, containing the elements lying between occurrences of a specified delimiter. A notion of correctness in this example involves expressing the function two ways (Figure 4), one of which is viewed as a correct specification, then verifying that the two definitions are extensionally equivalent.

Two lectures discuss a more extensive design and verification example: AVL trees (insertion, deletion, and search) expressed in about 130 lines of ACL2, with roughly the same number of additional lines devoted to stating lemmas and correctness properties. The theme of these lectures is designing correctness into software from the beginning by stating the properties each function is expected to have. Most of the properties in the AVL case have to do with preserving order, preserving or restoring balance, and conserving keys in various operations on trees.[1]

```
(defun packets (d xs)
  (if (atom xs)
      '(nil)
      (let* ((split (break-at d xs))
             (first-packet (car split))
             (rest (cadr split)))
        (cons first-packet
              (if (atom rest)
                  nil
                  (packets d (cdr rest)))))))
(defun packet-n (n d xs)
  (take-to d (drop-past-n-delimiters n d xs)))
(defthm packets-thm
  (implies
    (and (true-listp xs) (integerp n) (>= n 0))
    (equal (packet-n n d xs)
    (nth n (packets d xs)))))
```

Figure 4. Correctness of packets.

6. PROJECTS IN SE-I

Designing the software development projects for Software Engineering I involved a lot of care and experimentation. I wanted to give the students problems on which they could be successful, even though none of them had prior experience with ACL2 and few had experience in declarative programming. I wanted students not only to design and implement software, but also to succeed in using the computational logic of ACL2 to verify at least a few properties of their code.

Initially, I was not at all confident that I could design projects on the fly to meet these goals. Fortunately, I was able to organize a summer research program for undergraduate students in 2003 to try out some ideas. I designed ten software development projects, with theorems expressing software properties that I thought students could verify with ACL2, and set the students involved in the research program to work on them.

Not all of the projects were suitable as specified, but the students were able to modify requirements so that, in the end, we had a set of ten software engineering projects that we knew students could successfully complete. These were the projects assigned in the fall, 2003 offering of Software Engineering I.

To prepare for fall, 2004, I scrapped some of the problems, rearranged others, developed some new ones, and had a pair of undergraduate students work on the problems during the summer of 2004. The software development projects used in fall, 2004 emerged from the efforts and suggestions of these students.

This represents a great deal more than the usual preparatory work for putting together a problem set for a course. But, using a computational logic as a principal element of a software engineering course was new to me. It seemed wise to find out, ahead of time, whether or not students could solve the problems with a reasonable amount of effort.

Having gone through the process twice has convinced me that, in addition to the usual guidelines that instructors follow in putting together software development projects for students, there are two tricks to designing projects when ACL2 is the implementation language:

1. Make sure all input/output is file based.
2. Identify properties to be verified, and find proofs of those properties, using ACL2, before assigning them.

These observations eliminate the need for students to test the projects before assigning them in the course. However, it's still a lot of work. I have to write the functions involved in the software properties to be verified and work through proofs using ACL2. This is part of the burden of using ACL2 in a software engineering course. One might hope that the burden could be reduced in the future by sharing projects among instructors.

[1] The project is incomplete. All the necessary properties and many supporting lemmas are stated, but proofs of order, balance, and key-conservation properties are complete only for primitive operations, such as rotations. Full verification awaits proofs of similar properties for insertion and deletion.

Project 0. The first of the six individual projects gives the students a chance to learn basic mechanics of the ACL2 system and to gain a little experience in specifying computations in the form of equations rather than sequences of commands. It consists of four small problems that students are likely to be familiar with from other courses.

The assignment requires students to define ACL2 functions specifying the following computations: Newton's method for approximating square roots, reversing a list, set operations (eliminating duplicates from a list, set union, set intersection, and set difference), and the towers of Hanoi problem. Students are not required to state or prove any theorems in this first assignment.

Almost all students succeeded in all parts of this project. A few failed to get ACL2 to admit their function for Newton's method for square roots. ACL2 will not admit a function to its logic unless it can prove termination, and termination is a bit tricky for Newton's method. Since ACL2 deals only in full-precision, rational numbers, a square root function needs an extra argument specifying a desired accuracy. The function computes an iteration count from this argument, and terminates based on this count.

Project 1. The second project requires students to define functions that compute the mean and variance of a sequence of numbers and the frequency count of each number in the sequence. Students are required to prove that the frequency-count function delivers the same result for every permutation of the input sequence. An example in the ACL2 book [3] proves a similar property for a sorting function, and this gives students a leg up in the software-verification part of the project. Otherwise, the proof would probably be too hard at this stage.

All students succeeded in completing a working program for Project 1. About half were able to verify that the frequency-count function is invariant with respect to permutations of the input sequence. This is a tricky property to state, and not all students were able to dig the material on permutations out of the textbook on their own.

Project 2. In the third project, students define three functions to compute the nth Fibbonaci number (one using nested recursion, one using tail recursion, and one using Kepler's formula). They use the mechanized logic of ACL2 to verify that two of the functions (the nested recursion and the tail recursion) are equivalent, and they use a stopwatch to compare efficiency. Students also define nested and tail recursions for the Lucas sequence (Fibbonaci, generalized to arbitrarily specified starting values) and use ACL2 to prove that the Lucas sequence is non-decreasing if the starting values are nonnegative.

Finally, the students are required to write an analytic essay describing why they believe the approximation to the square root of five that their function uses in Kepler's formula is accurate enough to deliver the correct answer. They use their Newton's method program from the first project to approximate the square root, and they are allowed to assume that k^{th} iterate of Newton's method (starting from 2 as the zeroth iterate) delivers an approximation to the square root of five that is correct in the first 2^{k-1} decimal digits.

Most students got ACL2 to prove the equivalence of nested and tail recursions for Fibbonaci. About a quarter of the students succeeded in proving that their Lucas functions delivered non-decreasing sequences. This property is easier for ACL2 to deal with in terms of the Lucas implementation based on nested recursion. The tail recursive version complicates the proof. So, the trick is to choose the "simpler" of two equivalent functions when verifying properties, which isn't necessarily the more efficient implementation.

This approach is a good lesson for a general setting: Sometimes it is worth finding two representations of a function, one that specifies an efficient computation, and one that is more clearly correct. Then, use ACL2 to prove that the two representations are equivalent. Finally, verify correctness of the simpler function, and use the more efficient one in the running software.

One student (of nearly fifty) composed an essay with a first-rate analysis of the accuracy that Kepler's formula requires in the approximation to the square root of five to deliver the correct value for the nth Fibbonaci number. About two-thirds of the essays had some engineering value, but danced around the main point without finding a real solution, and the remaining third missed the point entirely.

Project 3. The fourth project involves producing a concordance of a text. The project gives syntactic rules defining words in the text and specifies line formats for the output file (requiring, for example, that the principal words appear in a column near the middle of the line, with the amount of surrounding context varying according to the size of the lines and the size of the principal word on the line).

The project calls for an *n log n* sorting function and a proof that it delivers a permutation of the input sequence in which the elements occur in increasing order. All students put together a working program for this project, and over three-quarters of them succeeded in getting ACL2 to prove the correctness of the sorting function (mostly following an example in the ACL2 book [3] of a similar theorem for an n^2 sorting function).

Project 4. The fifth project converts a file of text into two word-frequency tables, one arranged alphabetically and one in decreasing order of word frequency. The program must include a function that converts a sequence of numbers arranged in increasing (or decreasing) order into a sequence of "run frequencies" — that is, a sequence of ratios between the length of each contiguous block of identical numbers in a given, ordered sequence and the total number of elements in the given sequence. This function has the property that the sum of the ratios in the sequence it delivers is one, and the project requires verification of this property using ACL2's computational logic.

All but a few of the students completed the program and over half succeeded in proving the required software property. This was the first proof in which it was necessary for students to explore supporting lemmas to get the proof to go through, and a fifty-percent success rate was better than might be expected.

Project 5. The last individual software development project calls for a function that compares the number of tokens in a given ACL2 program with the number of tokens it would have if invocations of defined functions were in-lined.

The project requires students to use a supplied software package implementing AVL trees to record function bodies (or token counts and argument reference counts) keyed by function names for later look-up while going through the program. It also requires them to choose two properties of the program to verify with ACL2's mechanized logic.

Almost all students succeeded both in constructing a working program and in carrying out the proofs. However, most of them chose rather minimal properties to verify. There was a wide variety in the complexity of the submitted programs, varying from a few hundred lines to over a thousand. The short programs were better.

Team Project 1. The concordance project (Project 3) is actually divided into five parts:

1. planning and design,
2. design review,
3. initial implementation of revised design,
4. code review, and
5. final implementation of reviewed code.

Parts 1, 3, and 5 are individual projects, and parts 2 and 4 are team projects. In part 1, students convert the problem description into a design, on an individual basis. Then, in part 2, the teams meet, choose one of the designs at random, conduct a design review in a team session, and then revise the design. In part 3, individual students implement the revised design through the unit testing phase, but without integration testing. In part 4, the teams meet again, select one of the implementations at random, and conduct a code review. In part 5, individual students complete the implementation of the reviewed code.

The project provides students with opportunities to experience the benefits of design and code review and to practice interpersonal skills. Most students seem to enjoy the project, and it serves, too, the purpose of providing practice for the second team project, which is a more substantial software development effort.

Team Project 2. The larger of the two team software projects in Software Engineering I requires the implementation of stock market analysis software. The software processes a file of inquiries describing analytic computations of stock market data. The syntax of inquiries is rudimentary, and the computations are not complicated, but the data file, which contains market data for S&P 500 corporations, is massive.

The software invokes functions in an AVL package to record data from the file, on the fly, to improve the response time of inquiries. In addition to the AVL package, students are encouraged to incorporate code from earlier projects (for statistical calculations, for example).

In addition to the usual reports on planning, estimation, development time, testing, and defects, the project requires documentation explaining how to use the software. Plus, teams choose two important properties of their code suitable for an ACL2 proof, write a short analysis of the benefits that proving the property might provide, and outline an approach to a proof. Finally, they choose one of the properties and prove it in ACL2.

The project gives students experience in organizing and cooperating in a modest software effort. (Implementations run one to two thousand lines.) It would be enhanced by explicit requirements for testing regimes and a prescribed effort in verified properties focused on some important aspect of correctness.

7. SE-II

Software Engineering II is a project-based course required of all seniors (final-year students) in computer science. In the 2005 offering of this course, I formed seven teams [4] of five or six students each to carry out team projects. There were thirteen separate items that each team was required to deliver, culminating in a full implementation of a software product of moderate size (3,000 to 5,000 lines of code implementing an "image calculator" that takes a formula specifying a computation that applies image operations to a sequence of images and generates a new sequence of images transformed by the operations in the formula).

The thirteen deliverables are due on a more-or-less weekly basis throughout the semester and include such items as initial design and time estimates, engineering standard, detailed design, design and code review reports, product specs and installation guide, unit and integration test suites following a testing strategy, final design and code, meeting logs, and three presentations.

There is one individual project consisting of a compilation of weekly progress reports, plus PSP documents [2] and ACL2-proven properties for each component the individual contributed to the team's software product. These individual projects are typically about thirty pages long, although some are as short as twenty, and some as long as two hundred pages. Usually, but not always, the longer ones are better.

Because Software Engineering II is a senior project course, most class periods are devoted to meeting time for the teams to keep their projects on track. Four class meetings are devoted to team presentations, and two are devoted to formal lectures. Informal lectures occur occasionally throughout the course.

8. PROJECTS IN SE-II

Teams of students in Software Engineering II, spring 2005, built a program to carry out image transformations (filtering for feature enhancement, differencing for background removal, addition, scaling, etc) in combinations specified by formulas presented in a syntax based on lambda expressions. They delivered their projects in the form of thirteen separate items with due-dates spread throughout the sixteen-week semester.

After two weeks, teams completed high-level designs together with size and time estimates based on PSP data [2] collected during the first semester. Shortly afterward, they wrote engineering standards (document management procedures, design and code style sheets, testing procedures, etc). They worked on more detailed designs and estimates for the next three weeks. In the midst of this period, they conducted design reviews. They delivered completed designs and estimates in the sixth week, along with ten-minute, in-class presentations describing their plans. Five deliverables, six weeks.

For the next eight weeks, the teams worked on implementation. Along the way, they delivered code review reports, product specifications, and unit and integration test suites. Finally they delivered the code itself and a thirty-minute presentation covering specific points, such as software architecture, implementation problems and solutions, planned versus actual schedules, remaining implementation problems, and potential enhancements. The teams were instructed to address an audience consisting of engineering management familiar only with a short description of their software product's goals. Six engineering managers from industry attended the presentations, asked questions, and left the students (and instructor) with written comments and evaluations. Five more deliverables, eight more weeks.

During the last two weeks, in addition to making their thirty-minute product presentations in class, the teams worked on a test suite for the software product of another team (assigned in round-robin fashion), based on that team's product specification, and a ten-minute presentation of the results of applying the test suite. Testing had to follow a known and documented strategy of the team's choice, such as statistical use-based testing or software reliability engineering.

The final item of the team project is a meeting log. All but a few class periods are devoted to meeting time for the teams. Before each meeting, each team submits an agenda. During the meeting, they annotate their agendas with discussion notes and decisions. This collection of annotated agendas comprises the meeting log. Altogether, thirteen team deliverables in a period of sixteen weeks.

During development of the team's software product, individual students put together reports on each software element (one function or a few related functions) they contribute to the product. These reports begin with a description of the software element and its role in the team's software design. They continue with a PSP log (plans, estimates, design, time log, defect log, testing templates, code, and summaries [2]). Each report also states at least one proven property of the contributed software element along with a summary of a proof of the property using ACL2.

The collected reports form one section of the sole individual project of Software Engineering II. The other section of the report consists of the collection of weekly reports each student makes throughout the semester. Each team meets with the instructor once a week for twenty minutes to discuss progress and problems, and the individual weekly reports serve as one form of input for those meetings.

In spring 2005, individual reports varied from twenty pages to two hundred, and quality had a similar range. Only a few students failed to take the individual project seriously. Two students completely omitted proofs of software properties, and about two-thirds of the software properties stated and proven in the reports had no perceptible theme or significant relevance to overall software correctness.

Nevertheless, most reports were of good quality. Five were outstanding, with insights about software processes, good explanations of the roles of individual software elements in the team's software product, and significant, proven software properties.

9. RESULTS

I expected some complaints from students and from the five representatives from industry who attended presentations in Software Engineering II about the use of an unusual programming environment, ACL2, for a project course in software engineering. To my surprise, I got none from either quarter, and actually got positive support from one industry representative and several students. So, the idea of using a functional paradigm in software engineering was reasonably well accepted.

In past years there has been considerable whining from students about the record keeping required for PSP reports [2]. There was still some of that, but substantially less, possibly because we now use a tool to reduce the burden of keeping logs, making estimates, and recording data.

Based on conversations with individual students and on evaluations of projects they turned in, I believe that all seventy-six of the students who completed both Software Engineering I and II in the 2003-2004 and 2004-2005 academic years managed to learn enough about functional programming to be able to use it effectively in subsequent projects.

Of the thirty-eight students who completed both courses in 2004-2005, about thirty understand how to formulate theorems about software properties, and see some value in stating theorems about software properties. Twenty-five can use ACL2's mechanized logic to verify at least a few software properties. Between ten and fifteen students can formulate theorems that, together, verify a coherent theme of software correctness. About the same number would choose ACL2 or another functional language for a software project in the future, given the opportunity. Five students acquired competence in using the ACL2 mechanized logic well beyond expectations and would be able to use it effectively on their own in new projects without additional training.

10. WISHES

Students would gain a better impression of functional programming if they could see it compete in speed of performance with programs written in C. This might be possible if, once ACL2 has been used to verify correctness, students could compile their code with a good Common Lisp compiler and run it from the resulting executable module. It seems that this would be easy, since ACL2 is a subset of Common Lisp, but so far, I have failed to find a way to do get C-like performance from ACL2 code. This is an improvement that I would like to make in the future.

It would also be nice if ACL2 were higher order. It isn't, and won't be, which is sometimes burdensome from a programming point of view. Many students asked for this feature and were somewhat disappointed that it is not available. Ironically, in earlier software engineering courses in which students were using C++ and passing a function as an argument to another function would have been advantageous (as in numerical quadrature, for example), most students avoided higher order functions by passing in a switch and choosing from a fixed collection of functions.

So, they didn't use higher order functions when they could, and should have. Now that they can't, they want to. Of course, the students involved are different, and not all students fall into either category. That accounts for the difference, but it seems ironic, anyway.

It would be even nicer if ACL2 had convenient support for interactive, graphical user interfaces. This may be feasible, perhaps with some sort of inter-language facility. It is something I would like to look into in the future, but probably not for the upcoming academic year. If I'm lucky, maybe someone else will provide a GUI solution.

Interestingly, two of the seven teams in the 2005 edition of Software Engineering II built a Java framework for automatically invoking their ACL2 code inside a GUI framework, thus solving the GUI problem themselves, but at a high expense. The Java harness was about as large (in terms of lines of code) as the ACL2 code implementing the main computation.

Two improvements of the coverage of defect control that I plan to introduce in the coming year are expanded usage of specified strategies for testing and the use of specific tools for configuration management and defect databases. During the first semester, students will be involved in planning for these changes, and the best of what they discover will go into the processes and tools they use in the second semester. Discussing a more comprehensive model for software quality would also improve the course, but there is some risk that it would make the course so broad that students would fail to get the intense experience that is one of the course's strengths.

A few of the best students from Software Engineering II made some recommendations about expanding the coverage of techniques for getting ACL2 to prove theorems. They suggested discussions of hints, inductive measures, and rule classes for type prescriptions and elimination. The students dug these ideas out of the ACL2 documentation and made good use of them during the year. I expect other students will find the methods useful and plan to introduce them in the next offering of Software Engineering I.

Finally, I wish I had given more guidance about what types of software properties student teams should address in their implementations. Only two of seven teams found coherent themes for applying ACL2's mechanized logic to correctness issues for their software. One of these teams dealt mostly with data-type issues and interfaces, and the other went far enough to consider their software proven correct for most intents and purposes. I think more teams would have this type of success if the project write-up were more explicit about productive uses of mechanized logic in the project.

11. GUESSES

I believe a computational logic like ACL2, integrated into a software development environment, would provide practical benefits in commercial software projects today. Theorem proving is ready for prime time.

The software development process, in this mode, would include using the development environment's logic to state important software properties at the same time that test sequences are designed — that is, ahead of or along with coding. The properties would be proved, gradually, as a normal software development activity, in parallel with testing.

Unfortunately few software engineers are ready for mechanized logic. If educators incorporate products like ACL2 in courses, the next generation of graduates could begin to reap the benefits of functional programming, especially a benefit that the functional paradigm facilitates far more effectively than any other: using mechanized logic to engineer reliable software.

12. MATERIALS

A package of materials for Software Engineering I and II, as described in this report, including syllabuses, schedules, lecture notes, assignments, and supplied software is available at http://www.cs.ou.edu/~rlpage/SEcollab

13. ACKNOWLEDGMENTS

I want to thank the students enrolled in software engineering courses at the University of Oklahoma whose experiences provided much of the material of this report. Especially, I want thank Nic Grounds, Isaac Harley, Jeff Kilpatrick, James Murphy, Elizabeth Murray, Stephen Pitts, and Jeff Sapp for their help in the design of projects and Butch de Berry and Zach Francks for pushing through ACL2 proofs of correctness properties of rotations and other operations in an AVL-tree implementation. Ryan Shepherd built the PSP automation engine used in the course, and the students and I are grateful for that.

Mike Brown (SAIC), Tony Caruso (MRE), David Franke (Trilogy, retired), Shane Merz (MRE), Boyd Nolan (PE), Ken Parker (Risk Metrics), Roger Rowe (Solarc), and Sunny Sethi (Xyant) attended in-class presentations by student teams. In addition to providing students with insight on applying concepts learned in an educational setting to commercial software development projects and contributing an industrial management perspective to the proceedings, they took the lead in developing guidelines for presentations. The software engineering courses at OU have benefited greatly from their efforts.

I also want to thank Rich Didday of INDEC Systems for helping develop major projects for Software Engineering II, including the image calculator project described in Section 8. Finally, I want to thank J Moore, Matt Kaufmann, and Jared Davis of the University of Texas, Austin, for helping my students and me learn to apply ACL2 in software engineering projects.

This report is based on work supported by the National Science Foundation under Grant No. EIA 0082849. Any opinions, findings and conclusions or recommendations expressed in this material are those of the author and do not necessarily reflect the views of the National Science Foundation.

14. REFERENCES

[1] Felleisen, M., Findler, R. B., Flatt, M., and Krishnamurthi, S. *How to Design Programs*. MIT Press, 2001.

[2] Humphrey, W. S. *A Discipline for Software Engineering*, Addison Wesley, 1995.

[3] Kaufmann, M., Manolios, P., and Moore, J. S. *Computer Aided Reasoning: An Approach*. Kluwer Academic Publishers, 2000.

[4] Michaelsen, L. K., "Getting Started with Team Based Learning" in *Team-Based Learning: A Transformative Use of Small Groups*, Praeger, Michaelsen, L.K., Knight, A. B., and Fink, L.D. editors, Stylus Publishing, Sterling VA, 2002.

[5] Pressman, R. *Software Engineering: A Practitioner's Approach, 6th Edition*. McGraw-Hill, 2005.

[6] Sommerville, I. *Software Engineering, 7th Edition*. Pearson, 2004.

Author Index

Notes